ṢALĀT

The Muslim Prayer Book

2016

ISLAM INTERNATIONAL PUBLICATIONS LIMITED

ṢALĀT—The Muslim Prayer Book

First Published in U.K. in 1994
Reprinted with some changes in 1996, followed by several editions in different countries of the world.
Reprinted in UK in 2014
Present Edition published in UK in 2016

Published by:
Islam International Publications Ltd
Islamabad
Sheephatch Lane
Tilford, Surrey
United Kingdom GU10 2AQ

Printed in UK at:
Raqeem Press
Unit 3, Bourne Mill Business Park
Guildford Road,
Farnham, Surrey, GU9 9PS

ISBN: 978-1-184880-856-0

Contents

PUBLISHERS' NOTE vii

FOREWORD xi

CHAPTER ONE 1

1. OBLIGATION TO OFFER PRAYER 2
2. IMPORTANCE OF PRAYER 4
3. THE TIMING OF PRAYERS 8
4. CONDITIONS FOR PRAYER 10

ABLUTION 12

FACTORS WHICH RENDER AN ABLUTION INEFFECTIVE 16

SOME NOTEWORTHY DIFFERENCES OF OPINION AMONG DIFFERENT SCHOOLS OF JURISPRUDENCE. 17

BATH 18

1. In Case of Women 18

2. In Case of Men and Women 19

ADDITIONAL SITUATIONS WHERE A BATH IS ESSENTIAL 19

WATER 20

DRESS 20

COVERING THE HEAD FOR MEN 21

5. *ADHĀN* 21

THE METHOD OF SAYING THE *ADHĀN* 23

IQĀMAT (*IQĀMAH*) 26

NIYYAT (*NIYYAH*) 27

COMBINING PRAYERS 28

CHAPTER TWO 31

1. THE METHOD OF OFFERING PRAYER 31

DURŪD (*AṢṢALĀTU 'ALAN-NABĪ*) 48

INDIVIDUAL PRAYER 54

CONGREGATIONAL PRAYER 54

2. SOME OTHER POINTS TO BE REMEMBERED 56

3. REMEMBRANCE OF ALLAH AFTER CONCLUSION OF THE PRAYER 61

4. TYPES OF PRAYERS AND NUMBER OF *RAK'ĀT* 65

FARḌ PRAYERS 65

WĀJIB PRAYERS 66

ṢALĀTUL-VITR 66

SUNNAT PRAYERS 68

NAWĀFIL PRAYERS 68

5. *ṢALĀTUL-JUMU'AH* or FRIDAY PRAYER 70

6. *'ĪDUL-FIṬR* AND *'ĪDUL-AḌḤĀ* FESTIVALS 74

7. CONSTITUENT PARTS OF PRAYER 78

FARḌ (COMPULSORY) PARTS OF PRAYER 78

WĀJIBĀT (ESSENTIALS) OF THE *ṢALĀT* 79

SUNAN (PLURAL OF *SUNNAT*) OF THE *ṢALĀT* 81

MUSTAḤIBBĀT OF THE *ṢALĀT* 82

MAKRŪHĀT OF THE *ṢALĀT* (UNDESIRABLE ACTS DURING PRAYER) 83

ACTIONS WHICH MAKE PRAYER NULL AND VOID 85

SUJŪDUS-SAHV, i.e. PROSTRATIONS OF CONDONEMENT 85

8. PRAYER OFFERED IN EXCEPTIONAL CIRCUMSTANCES 86

PRAYER DURING SICKNESS 86

PRAYER DURING A JOURNEY 87
PRAYER DURING DANGER (*ṢALĀTUL-KHAUF*) 89
QAḌĀ (MISSED) PRAYERS 89
TAHAJJUD PRAYER 90
TARĀVĪḤ PRAYER 91
PRAYER WHEN SOLAR AND LUNAR ECLIPSES OCCUR 92
PRAYER TO INVOKE RAIN 93
ISTIKHĀRAH PRAYER 94
ṢALĀTUL-ḤĀJJĀT, i.e. PRAYERS OFFERED WHEN IN NEED OF HELP 96
ISHRĀQ PRAYER 98
FUNERAL PRAYER 98
PRAYER FOR A DECEASED MALE CHILD 102
PRAYER FOR A DECEASED FEMALE CHILD 103
Glossary of Terms 107

PUBLISHERS' NOTE

The name of Muhammad, the Holy Prophet[sa] of Islam, has been followed by the symbol [sa], which is an abbreviation for the salutation *Ṣallallāhu 'Alaihi Wasallam* (may peace and blessings of Allah be upon him). The names of other Prophets and Messengers are followed by the symbol [as], an abbreviation for *'Alaihis-Salām* (on whom be peace). The actual salutations have not generally been set out in full, but they should nevertheless, be understood as being repeated in full in each case. The symbol [ra] is used with the name of the companions of the Holy Prophet[sa] and those of the Promised Messiah[as]. It stands for *Raḍiyallāhu 'anhu/'anha/'anhum* (may Allah be pleased with him/with her/with them). [rh] stands for *Raḥimahullāhu Ta'ālā* (may Allah have mercy on him). [at] stands for *Ayyadahullāhu Ta'ālā* (may Allah be his Helper).

In transliterating Arabic words we have followed the following system adopted by the Royal Asiatic Society.

ا at the beginning of a word, pronounced as *a*, *i*, *u*.

ث *th*, pronounced like *th* in the English word 'thing'.

ح *ḥ*, a guttural aspirate, stronger than *h*.

خ *kh*, pronounced like the Scotch *ch* in 'loch'.

ذ *dh*, similar to the English *th* in 'this' or 'that'. This is not the exact sound. Its pronunciation must be learnt by the ear.

ص *ṣ*, strongly articulated *s*.

ض *ḍ*, similar to the English *th* in 'this' or 'that'. This is not the exact sound. Its pronunciation must be learnt by the ear.

ط *ṭ*, strongly articulated palatal *t*.

ظ *ẓ*, strongly articulated *z*.

ع ‘, a strong guttural, the pronunciation of which must be learnt by the ear.

غ *gh*, a sound approached very nearly in the *r* '*grasseye*' in French, and in the German *r*. It requires the muscles of the throat to be in the 'gargling' position whilst pronouncing it.

ق *q*, a deep guttural *k* sound.

ء ’, a sort of catch in the voice.

Short vowels are represented by:

a for ـَـ (like *u* in 'bud');

i for ـِـ (like *i* in 'bid');

u for ـُـ (like *oo* in 'wood');

Long vowels by:

ā for ـــاـــ or آ (like *a* in 'father');

ī for ی ـــِـــ or ـــٖـــ (like *ee* in 'deep');

ū for و ـــُـــ (like *oo* in 'root');

Other:

ai for ی ـــَـــ (like *i* in 'site')♦;

au for و ـــَـــ (resembling *ou* in 'sound').

Please note that in transliterated words the letter 'e' is to be pronounced as in 'prey' which rhymes with 'day'; however the pronunciation is flat without the element of English diphthong. If in Urdu and Persian words 'e' is lengthened a bit more it is transliterated as 'ei' to be pronounced as 'ei' in 'feign' without the element of diphthong thus 'کے' is transliterated as 'Kei'. For the nasal sound of 'n' we have used the symbol 'ń'. Thus Urdu word 'میں' is transliterated as 'meiń'.*

The consonants not included in the above list have the same phonetic value as in the principal languages of Europe.

♦ In Arabic words like شَیخ (Shaikh) there is an element of diphthong which is missing when the word is pronounced in Urdu.

* These transliterations are not included in the system of transliteration by Royal Asiatic Society. [Publishers]

We have not transliterated Arabic words which have become part of English language, e.g., Islam, Mahdi, Quran**, Hijra, Ramadan, Hadith, ulema, umma, sunna, kafir, pukka etc.

For quotes straight commas (straight quotes) are used to differentiate them from the curved commas used in the system of transliteration, ‘ for ع, ’ for ء. Commas as punctuation marks are used according to the normal usage. Similarly for apostrophe normal usage is followed.

The Publishers

** Concise Oxford Dictionary records Quran in three forms—Quran, Qur’an and Koran. [Publishers]

FOREWORD

The Institute of Islam International Publications Ltd. is rendering unprecedented services in the field of publicising accurate Islamic teachings and is engaged day and night in producing books for the spiritual uplift of mankind. As a proof here is a new publication;

ṢALĀT - THE MUSLIM PRAYER BOOK

Prayer, in every religion is regarded as the pivot on which rests man's Communion with God. God prescribed prayer as the second pillar of His everlasting religion ISLAM.

In this modern materialistic world such books can serve as satisfying spiritual food for the starving souls and as such are the need of this age. With many people coming into the fold of Islam this book can certainly be a source of explaining to them all the aspects of the congregational prayer.

Although some other booklets on the subject are available, they are not so comprehensive and explanatory. In addition to detailed word-pictures about the significance of prayer, combined with Arabic text, its transliteration and translation, all the postures have been demonstrated with pictures. The postures in prescribed prayer play a very important role in the proper performance as they represent the real state of mind of the worshipper in the presence of God. All these postures are divinely taught.

Another landmark of the book is the all-exhaustive description of each and every kind of Islamic prayer, obligatory or non-obligatory so that the reader is not left looking for some other help in connection with the Islamic prayers.

This book is the need of the time and should be possessed by every Muslim family.

The Publishers

CHAPTER ONE

The purpose of the creation of man, according to Islam, is that he should worship Allah. Allah says in the Holy Quran:

وَمَا خَلَقْتُ الْجِنَّ وَالْإِنْسَ إِلَّا لِيَعْبُدُوْنِ

And I have not created the Jinn and the men but that they may worship Me. (51:57)

Worship means total obedience to the commands of Allah. The Holy Prophet Muhammad[sa] brought the message of God and explained all the commandments concerning the religion of Islam.

Islam has five basic duties which a Muslim has to perform. They are known as the Five Fundamentals of Islam or the Five Pillars of Islam.

The first pillar of Islam is the Islamic declaration of faith, i.e. to bear witness that there is none worthy of worship except Allah, and that Muhammad is the Messenger of Allah. The oneness of God is the basis of our belief in Islam.

The second pillar is called *Ṣalāt*, i.e. to perform Prayer in a prescribed form.

The third pillar is called *Zakāt,* a form of levy which Muslims of means pay annually in cash or kind, and is spent for good causes mentioned in the Holy Quran.

The fourth pillar is called *Ṣaum*, i.e. to keep fasts in the month of Ramadan.

The fifth pillar is called *Ḥajj*, i.e. to perform

pilgrimage to the *Ka'bah* in Mecca least once in the lifetime of a Muslim.

Of all religious obligations, Islam has laid greatest emphasis on the institution of *Ṣalāt*. It is enjoined upon every Muslim to pray five times a day. Besides the five obligatory Prayers, there are other types of Prayers which are optional.

A Muslim takes the spiritual side of life as seriously as a worldly person takes the material side of it. As air and food are essential for our physical life, likewise, we cannot survive spiritually without offering *Ṣalāt* or Prayer regularly in different parts of the day.

Ṣalāt or Prayer, consists of various postures, i.e. Standing called *Qiyām*, Bowing down called *Rukū'*, Prostration called *Sajdah* and Sitting called *Qa'dah*. During each posture prescribed phrases are to be recited. As these phrases are in Arabic, every Muslim is required not only to memorise these verses but also to know their meaning so that the worshipper knows what he is saying to his Lord during the Prayer.

1. OBLIGATION TO OFFER PRAYER

Prayer, in the prescribed manner, is obligatory upon every adult Muslim of sound mind. As far as children are concerned, it is not obligatory on them until they come of age. However, it requires continuous effort and persuasion to get them to the stage where they start offering their Prayers regularly in the manner prescribed for the Prayer. Proper training and education is therefore necessary for children. It is for this reason that the Holy Prophet[sa] has directed that when children reach the age of seven, parents should urge them to be regular in their Prayers and when they reach the age of ten, they must be admonished if they fail to offer their Prayers regularly. (*Sunan Abū Dāwūd, Kitābuṣ-Ṣalāt*).

Once the children reach the age of maturity, it becomes compulsory for them to offer their Prayers. At that stage, no individual or Government has the right to force them to offer their Prayers, as the *Ṣalāt* offered under compulsion does not mean anything. It ought to be offered willingly. The matter rests between the person and his God. Therefore, it is the duty of every and all Muslim parents to prepare their children for *Ṣalāt* from an early age. Moreover, it is highly essential for them to pray to God Almighty that their children become regular in Prayers. God's help is sought because the task is huge.

It is mentioned in the Holy Quran that throughout his life Ḥaḍrat Ishmael[as] used to exhort members of his household to offer their Prayers regularly. It is often observed that in homes where elders offer their Prayers regularly, the children start copying the movements of their elders naturally and thus become regular in their Prayers, with time. However, when a child reaches the age of seven, the proper method of Prayer should be taught to him. He should be encouraged to join in Prayer and, if possible, he should be persuaded to accompany the parents to the mosque. This will develop in the child an affinity with Prayer, and will safeguard the habit of Prayer in the following generation. The parent or guardian, however, is permitted to be somewhat strict with the children between the ages of 10 to 12, should they become slack in offering their Prayers. This does not mean that they should be treated cruelly or punished, rather they should be admonished to the same degree as parents often admonish them for missing school. However, when they reach the age of twelve, they should be made to realise that their parents have discharged their duty and from that time on, the matter rests between them and God, to Whom they are answerable. This does not mean that they should not be advised, exhorted or admonished because as far as advising them is concerned, it can go on for life, if required. It is only the element of strictness which comes to an end when the child reaches the age of twelve. As mentioned earlier, Ḥaḍrat Ishmael[as] adopted the same method of love and kind persuasion with the members of his household. The Holy Prophet Muhammad[sa] treated the grown-ups in his family in the same manner. It is reported that he used to call out to his daughter Ḥaḍrat Fāṭimah[ra] and his son-in-law Ḥaḍrat 'Alī[ra] to wake them up for *Fajr* Prayer.

2. IMPORTANCE OF PRAYER

Ṣalāt or the prescribed Prayer has been mentioned in the Holy Quran as an essential characteristic of a true believer. The Holy Quran states:

ذٰلِكَ الْكِتٰبُ لَا رَيْبَ ۛ فِيْهِ ۛ هُدًى لِّلْمُتَّقِيْنَ ۙ الَّذِيْنَ

يُؤْمِنُوْنَ بِالْغَيْبِ وَ يُقِيْمُوْنَ الصَّلٰوةَ وَ مِمَّا رَزَقْنٰهُمْ

يُنْفِقُوْنَ ۝

This is a perfect Book; there is no doubt in it; it is *a guidance for the righteous, Who believe in the unseen and observe Prayer, and spend out of what We have provided for them;* (2:3-4)

Prayer or *Ṣalāt*, helps us to get rid of sins; inclines us more and more towards God and goodly things and so gradually purifies us. But this is not the end. Prayer does much more than this. It brings man closer to his Creator. The worshipper tries to imitate God in His most excellent attributes and is constantly transformed from a lowly and worldly person to a highly noble and sublime servant of God. The Holy Quran mentions this distinctive quality of *Ṣalāt* by saying:

اُتْلُ مَآ اُوْحِيَ اِلَيْكَ مِنَ الْكِتٰبِ وَ اَقِمِ الصَّلٰوةَ ؕ اِنَّ الصَّلٰوةَ

تَنْهٰى عَنِ الْفَحْشَآءِ وَ الْمُنْكَرِ ؕ وَ لَذِكْرُ اللّٰهِ اَكْبَرُ ؕ وَ اللّٰهُ يَعْلَمُ

مَا تَصْنَعُوْنَ ۝

Recite that which has been revealed to thee of the Book, and observe Prayer. Surely, Prayer restrains one *from indecency and manifest evil, and remembrance of Allah indeed is the greatest* virtue. *And Allah knows what you do.* (29:46)

Prayer is indeed a sure and well-tried prescription

for purity of the heart and the soul. It is through *Ṣalāt* alone that we are able to establish a living communion with Allah. The Quran says:

اِنَّ الَّذِيْنَ يَتْلُوْنَ كِتٰبَ اللّٰهِ وَ اَقَامُوا الصَّلٰوةَ وَ اَنْفَقُوْا
مِمَّا رَزَقْنٰهُمْ سِرًّا وَّ عَلَانِيَةً يَّرْجُوْنَ تِجَارَةً لَّنْ تَبُوْرَ ۙ
لِيُوَفِّيَهُمْ اُجُوْرَهُمْ وَ يَزِيْدَهُمْ مِّنْ فَضْلِهٖ ؕ اِنَّهٗ غَفُوْرٌ
شَكُوْرٌ ۝

Surely, only *those who follow the Book of Allah and observe Prayer and spend out of what We have provided for them, secretly and openly, hope for a bargain which will never fail; In order that He may give them their full rewards, and* even *increase them out of His bounty. He is surely Most Forgiving, Most Appreciating. (35:30-31)*

According to the Holy Prophet[sa] *Ṣalāt* is the pinnacle of the spiritual life of the believer. It is the highest form of Divine worship. The Holy Prophet[sa] is further reported to have observed:

Prayer brings the believer into communion with his Lord.

It must be realised that sincere prayer never goes in vain. Sometimes, the deep spiritual experience of the intense love of God brings tears to the eyes. Sometimes, a milder pleasure of love fills the heart with sublime happiness. These experiences are signs of the Prayer being alive, meaningful and fruitful. Otherwise, just a performance of formality is not enough to benefit man. That would be obeying an order without one's heart being in it. That is why it is highly essential that every beginner should keep this noble objective before him and always try to make his Prayers come alive.

The *Ṣalāt* combines all forms and degrees expressive of humility and submission. The worshippers stand in rows and respectfully behind the *Imām*.

All the worshippers who line up behind the *Imām* must follow his movements at his call. The call for every movement is *Allāhu Akbar* except when the *Imām* straightens himself from the position of *Rukū'*, i.e. the bowing position, when instead of saying *Allāhu Akbar*, he says *Sami'allāhu Liman Ḥamidah* which means 'most certainly God listens to those who praise Him.' At this call, all the followers also straighten up with arms by their sides, saying *Rabbanā Wa Lakal Ḥamd, Ḥamdan Kathīran Ṭayyiban Mubārakan Fīhi.*

Sincerity and humility are the essence of prayer. Allah enjoins believers:

قَدْ اَفْلَحَ الْمُؤْمِنُوْنَ ۝ الَّذِيْنَ هُمْ فِيْ صَلَاتِهِمْ خٰشِعُوْنَ ۝

Surely, success does come to the believers, Who are humble in their Prayers, (23:2-3)

The Holy Prophet[sa] has said: *No servant of Allah humbles himself for the sake of Allah, but Allah thereby brings about his Raf'a. Raf'a* is an Arabic word meaning 'to raise'. It does not mean that Allah will lift him bodily to heaven. Obviously it means that Allah will exalt his status before Him.

True humility can only be achieved by mentally concentrating on the attributes of Allah. When His immense greatness dawns on someone, one has no choice but to be humbled.

3. THE TIMING OF PRAYERS

For each of the five obligatory Prayers, there is an appointed time fixed in relation to the sun's position.

The time of the *Fajr* or morning Prayer begins with dawn and ends just before sunrise.

The time of the *Ẓuhr* or midday Prayer begins after the sun has crossed the zenith point and has begun to decline.

The time of the *'Aṣr* Prayer is when the sun has further advanced in decline and reaches a point nearly halfway between the beginning of decline and sunset, which we may call late afternoon but not very late. It ends up quite some time before sunset, when the sunlight has paled. Although it is not entirely forbidden to say the *'Aṣr* Prayer that late in the day, it is most certainly preferred that it be offered before daylight has started fading out while the sun is still above the horizon by a good measure.

It is to be remembered that at the times of sunrise,

sunset and when the sun is at its zenith, it is forbidden to offer Prayers. Also, when the *'Aṣr* Prayer has been performed, no optional Prayer should be offered between that time and the time of sunset. Similarly, between morning Prayer and sunrise no optional Prayer should be offered.

The time of *Maghrib* Prayer begins immediately after the sun has set. It lasts till dusk. But the word dusk is differently understood by the different schools of Jurists. The *Wahhābīs* and similar sects with a rigid attitude insist that *Maghrib* Prayer should be offered almost immediately after sunset and that the time of dusk, according to them, ends when the redness of the sunset gives way to a dusky grey. Many other sects believe that dusk lasts still when there is some light left on the horizon after sunset. According to such schools, the allotted time for offering *Maghrib* Prayer is almost as long as that allotted for performing morning Prayer which lasts from early dawn to sunrise.

All schools of jurisprudence agree that the time for the *'Ishā'* Prayer begins when dusk has finally disappeared, giving way to the darkness of night. According to most, this period lasts till midnight but some even extend it beyond midnight till one retires for sleep. It is, however, very strongly advised and preferred that Prayers should be generally offered at the beginning of their respective times and should not be delayed until the time is about to run out.

4. CONDITIONS FOR PRAYER

Some prerequisites and conditions exist regarding the offering of Prayers. They are as follows:

i. Determination of Intention: The intention to perform a Prayer must be made prior to the beginning of the Prayer.

ii. The Prayer should be offered within the fixed time allotted for that particular Prayer. However, it should be remembered that if one fails to perform a Prayer in time due to some compelling reasons, that Prayer can be offered whenever one remembers it. However, it should not be offered at forbidden times. The question arises that if the timings for Prayer and fasting, etc., are associated with the duration of sunlight, with the rotation of the earth and the relative position of the sun and moon, how could one determine the timings of Prayer and fasting in extreme Southern and Northern areas where the duration of days and nights are longer than twenty-four hours? It should be noted that the Holy Prophet[sa] replying to a question from a Companion, explained that in those areas where the days and nights are of longer duration as compared to the normal 24-hour day, Muslims should offer their Prayers by measuring time in accordance with the normal length of a day.

iii. One should be clean in body and, as far as possible, in mind and spirit also. Cleanliness here is a term which means:

a. The body should be clean from all filth.
b. If one has answered the call of nature and has been to the toilet, one should wash oneself properly so that all remnants of faeces or urine have been properly washed away.
c. After conjugation, whether ejaculation has taken place or not or when, in whatever manner, ejaculation has taken place, for instance during sleep, cleanliness would mean not just washing oneself partially, but a full bath becomes essential.
d. A full bath is also essential for women after menstruation, and after post-parturition bleeding (bleeding following childbirth).

iv. The place and mat of Prayer must be neat and clean.

v. The body must be properly covered during the Prayer.

vi. *Qiblah* or Direction: All Muslims must face towards the *Ka'bah*. *Qiblah* means facing the *Ka'bah* in Makkah, the first House of worship built on earth.

All Muslims throughout the world should always face the general direction of the *Ka'bah* during every Prayer. However, during a journey and when travelling, if one fails to determine the direction properly or when one is unable to face towards the *Ka'bah* because of illness, for it is beyond one's capacity to do so, then one is not obliged to face towards the *Qiblah*. Also, when on a journey, riding on a mount, train, boat or plane, one should say one's Prayers facing in the same direction towards which one is moving, or indeed any convenient position will be acceptable.

ABLUTION

The word ablution applies to washing some parts of the body preparatory to the performance of Prayer. This is a prerequisite which must be fulfilled, otherwise the Prayer will not be considered valid. The Hadith clearly instructs that one should wash one's hands three times with water and then clean one's mouth by rinsing with water three times.

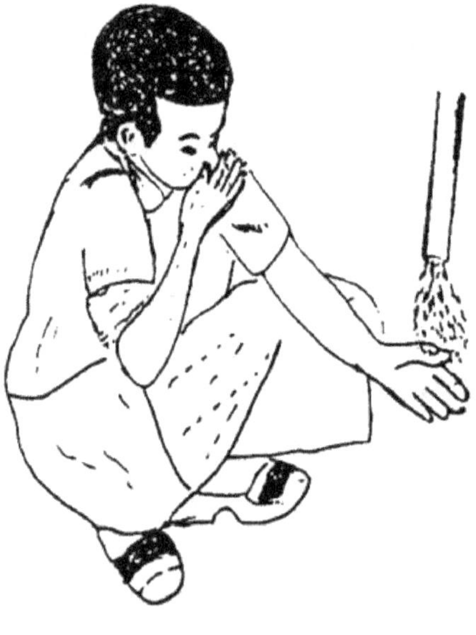

Then, the nose should be internally cleaned by pushing a little water into the nostrils three times.

And then the entire face should be washed three times.

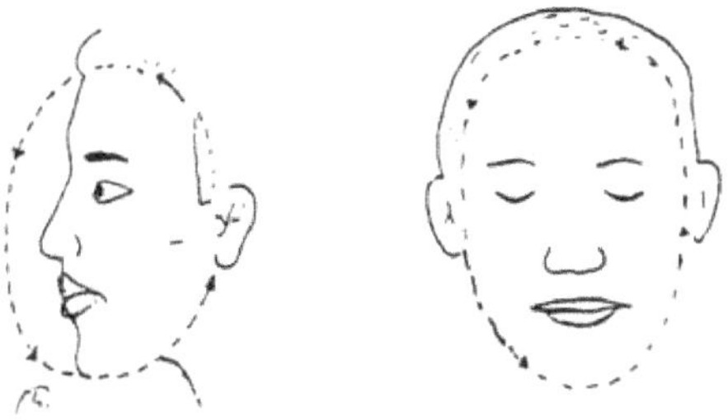

After this, the whole of the forearm up to and including the elbow should be washed three times each, starting with the right.

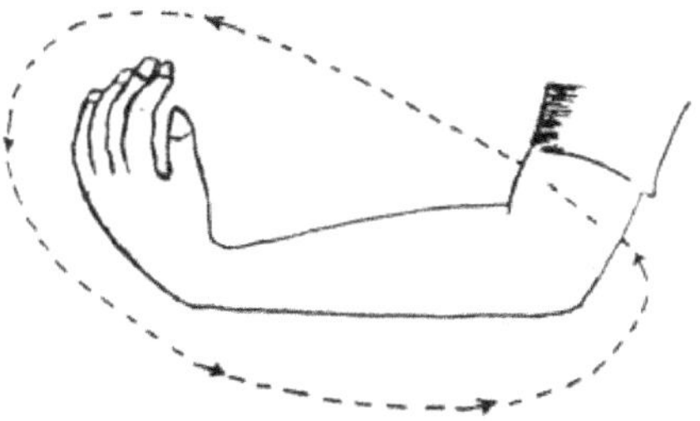

Then, having wetted the hands with some water again, a pass should be made over the head with both hands, palms downwards with thumbs outstretched so that almost the whole head is covered by this in a passing motion. At the end of this motion, the ears should be cleaned with the tips of the forefingers. The forefinger of the right hand is used for the right ear and the forefinger of the left hand is used for the left ear. The finger tips move along the crevices and grooves of the outside ear and are dipped slightly into the ear holes.

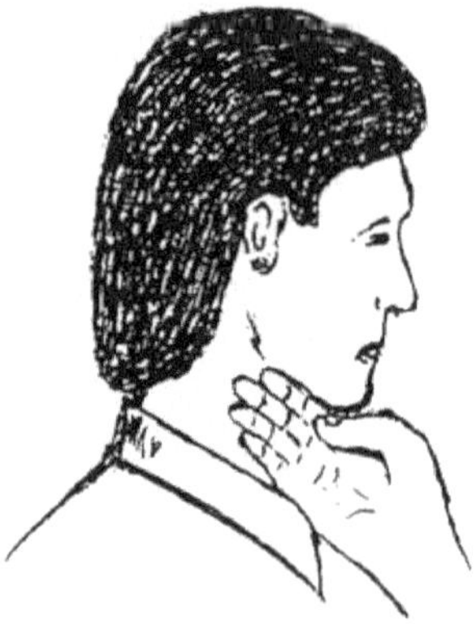

After passing the finger tips around the grooves of the external ear and dipping them into the ear holes, all fingers are joined together and the hands are inverted so that the palms now are facing outwards. With the back of the hands, a pass is made from the nape of the neck to the front of the neck.

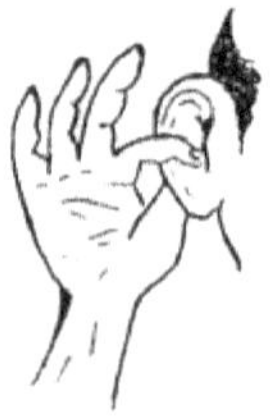

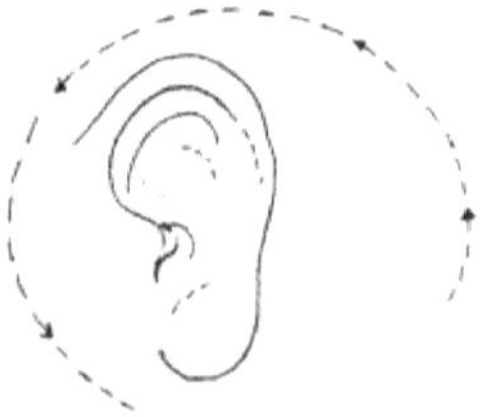

Lastly the feet should be washed up to the ankles inclusive, three times each, again beginning with the right. If for some reason, the limbs are washed just once, or twice, during the ablution, the ablution is still complete, even though the best form of ablution is that which we find in the established *Sunnah* of the Holy Prophet Muhammad[sa] which is to wash the limbs three times. Thus the ablution is completed.

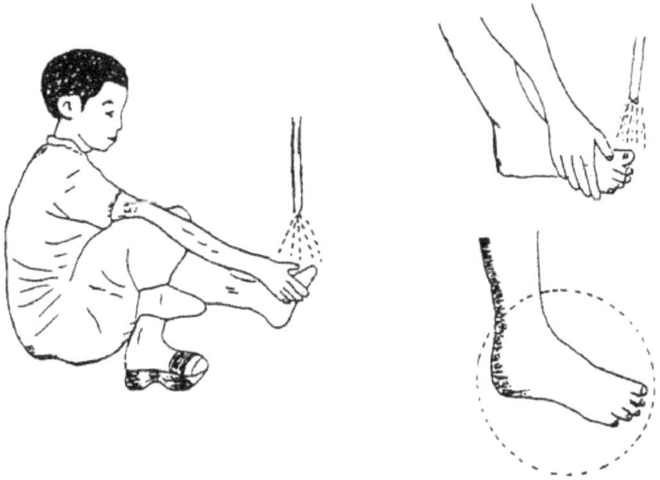

It is essential that the following prescribed prayer be recited for ablution:

اَللّٰهُمَّ اجْعَلْنِيْ مِنَ التَّوَّابِيْنَ وَاجْعَلْنِيْ مِنَ الْمُتَطَهِّرِيْنَ

Transliteration:

Allāhummaj'alnī minat-tawwābīna waj'alnī minal mutaṭahhirīn.

Translation:

O Allah make me of those who seek forgiveness and make me of those who are cleansed.

This is ablution in normal circumstances when one is healthy and the use of water is not medically inadvisable, and where clean water is easily available. In case of illness or non-availability of water, there is a simple substitute for ablution in the following form which is called *Tayammum.*

If a clean dusty surface or a solid surface is available, one should pat the surface with the open palms of both hands, and make a motion with both hands passing them over one's face. Then, one should pass the hands over the back of each other successively. If too much dust accumulates on the hands, then one is permitted to dislodge the excess. This is only a token ablution to remind one that whenever possible, proper ablution should be performed.

It is essential that one should offer Prayer while one's ablution is intact. If one's ablution remains intact then even with one ablution, more than one Prayer can be performed. This means that the state of ablution is necessary when one performs Prayer but for each Prayer repetition of ablution is not necessary if the previous ablution is still valid.

FACTORS WHICH RENDER AN ABLUTION INEFFECTIVE

a. Passing wind.

b. Urination even if a drop has passed out.

c. Passing stool in however small quantity.

d. Sleeping, dozing off to the degree that if one were

without a support, one would not be able to keep balance.

e. Menstruation and ejaculation, which have already been discussed earlier.

f. About vomiting and bleeding, opinions are divided but minor bleeding from any part of the body by an ordinary cut, etc., or throwing-up of a little food during belching should not be counted as bleeding and vomiting. Otherwise, after vomiting and bleeding, ablution should be performed again.

If after ablution, one puts on socks, then it is not essential to wash one's feet for the following 24 hours when one performs ablution. Instead, one should wet one's hands and after shaking off the excess water, one should make passes with the hands on both feet on top of the socks. This should be considered an alternative to the washing of the feet. This permission is extended to three days during a journey.

SOME NOTEWORTHY DIFFERENCES OF OPINION AMONG DIFFERENT SCHOOLS OF JURISPRUDENCE

According to *Shia* jurisprudence, the feet are exempted from washing and only the passes as mentioned before are enough, whether one is wearing socks or not. According to some more rigid schools of thought like the *Wahhābīs*, ordinary socks, whether they be woollen or cotton are not enough. Socks have to be made of thin leather which is impervious to dust and moisture, etc., in order to avail of such concession.

According to some other schools, this attitude is too strict and makes one slave to superficialities which is not in the true spirit of Islam. The Holy Prophet[sa] described the spirit of Islam by saying:

إِنَّ الدِّيْنَ يُسْرٌ

Transliteration:

Innaddīna Yusrun.

Translation:

Indeed it is a religion of ease. (*Bukhārī, Kitābul-Īmān*)

The Ahmadiyya Muslim Community agree with this. They consider the best policy is to apply common sense. So, if a pair of socks are thick enough to protect one's feet from dirt and filth, the question of which material they are made of does not arise.

BATH

Taking a bath is always encouraged and promoted in Islam. Islam emphasises not only the cleanliness of the soul but also that of the body. In some situations however, it has been made a prerequisite to the offering of any formal Prayer. The following are the conditions which necessitate taking a bath and where ablution alone is not enough.

1. In Case of Women

a. After each menstruation when the flow of blood has completely stopped.

b. After childbirth when the bleeding has finally stopped.

   Note: During these bleeding periods, women are not required to perform formal Prayers.

2. In Case of Men and Women

a. After seminal ejaculation or orgasm, whether resulting from conjugation or from any other cause. The same applies to night discharges during sleep.
b. Sexual contact between man and woman, even without ejaculation and however brief it may be.
c. All non-Muslims who become Muslims are also obliged to take a bath and start a new, fresh life as a Muslim.

ADDITIONAL SITUATIONS WHERE A BATH IS ESSENTIAL

Every new born child must be bathed, and also the body of every person who has died should be bathed before the *Janāzah* Prayer. However, for those who are martyred or killed during war or murdered in any way, an exception is made and they are not bathed.

Apart from the occasions when bathing becomes necessary, the taking of a bath every Friday, on the celebrations of *'Īd* and just before performing *Ḥajj* were strongly emphasised by the Holy Prophet[sa].

It is interesting to note that the Holy Founder[sa] of Islam used to take a bath in the following manner:

He would start bathing by performing *Wuḍū'*, i.e. ablution, but not including washing of the feet which he would do at the end. Then he would pour water at least three times on the right side of his body, followed by three times on the left. He bathed so meticulously that every pore of every part of his body was washed thoroughly.

In all such conditions where bathing becomes obligatory, one can neither perform Prayer without bathing nor enter the mosque, nor recite the Holy Quran. Exception is made for women during their periods as far as the reading of the Holy Quran is concerned. They can read the Holy Quran but are advised not to touch it with their bare hands.

WATER

Water to be used for ablution and bathing should be clean and salubrious. Stagnant or polluted water may not be used. However, when salubrious water is not available and people are forced to use whatever water is available, the same can also be used for ablution and bath.

DRESS

During Prayer, one's body should be decently covered, particularly the private parts and the areas around them. In case of men, this can be defined as an area of body beginning from the navel down to the end of the knee-cap. As far as women are concerned, they should cover their entire body, including their arms but excluding the hands and feet. However, when praying at home or among other women, they do not have to cover their faces.

COVERING THE HEAD FOR MEN

According to most schools of Jurisprudence, men should cover their heads when praying. But the *Mālikīs* and a few others do not consider this necessary.

5. *ADHĀN*

In the early days of Islam, there was no prescribed way of telling people that the time for Prayer had commenced nor was there any means to call the Muslims to the mosque for congregational Prayers. The Holy Prophet[sa] was however, aware of the Jewish, Christian and pagan practices in this regard. He sought counsel and asked his Companions as to what should be done to call Muslims to the mosque for congregational Prayers. One morning, Ḥaḍrat 'Abdullāh ibn 'Azīz[ra] approached the Holy Prophet[sa] and related to him a dream which he had had the night before. He had seen someone announcing the Prayer time and calling people to the mosque for the congregational Prayer in a loud voice. Ḥaḍrat 'Abdullāh then related the words of the *Adhān* which he had heard in the dream. They were as follows:

اَللّٰہُ اَکْبَرُ

Transliteration:

Allāhu Akbar (four times)

Translation:

Allah is the Greatest. (Recited four times)

اَشْهَدُ اَنْ لَّا اِلٰهَ اِلَّا اللّٰه

Transliteration:

Ashhadu allā ilāha illallāh (twice)

Translation

I bear witness that there is none worthy of worship except Allah. (Recited twice)

اَشْهَدُ اَنَّ مُحَمَّدًا رَّسُوْلُ اللّٰه

Transliteration:

Ashhadu anna Muḥammadar Rasūlullāh (twice)

Translation:

I bear witness that Muhammad is the Messenger of Allah. (Recited twice)

حَیَّ عَلَی الصَّلٰوۃ

Transliteration:

Ḥayya ʻalaṣ-Ṣalāḥ (twice)

Translation:

Come to Prayer. (Recited twice)

حَیَّ عَلَی الْفَلَاح

Transliteration:

Ḥayya 'alal-Falāḥ (twice)

Translation:

Come to success.(Recited twice)

اَللّٰهُ اَكْبَرُ

Transliteration:

Allāhu Akbar (twice)

Translation:

Allah is the Greatest.(Recited twice)

لَا اِلٰهَ اِلَّا اللّٰه

Transliteration:

Lā ilāha illallāh

Translation:

There is none worthy of worship except Allah.

Ḥaḍrat 'Umar[ra], who later became the second *Khalīfah* was also sitting in the company of the Holy Prophet[sa]. He said that he had also had a dream and had heard the same words. The Holy Prophet[sa] was therefore in no doubt that this was a message from Allah, so he adopted the method of *Adhān* to call worshippers to the mosque. *Adhān* is thus widely recognised as the call to Prayer all over the world.

THE METHOD OF SAYING THE *ADHĀN*

The *Mu'adhdhin*, the person who says the *Adhān*,

should stand in a prominent position with his face turned towards the *Qiblah*. These days a loudspeaker system is also used to say the *Adhān*. The *Mu'adhdhin* should touch his ears with his index fingers, right finger touching the right ear and the left finger touching the left, and recite the *Adhān* in a loud voice. He should turn his face towards the right when saying the words, *Ḥayya 'alaṣ-Ṣalāh* and turn his face to the left while reciting the words *Ḥayya 'alal-Falāḥ*.

During the *Adhān* for *Fajr* Prayer, the *Mu'adhdhin* should also recite the words given below twice after saying, *Ḥayya 'alal-Falāḥ*:

اَلصَّلٰوةُ خَيْرٌ مِّنَ النَّوْمِ

Transliteration:

Aṣṣalātu khairum-minan-naum (twice)

Translation:

Prayer is better than sleep.(Recited twice)

The Holy Prophet[sa] has said:

إِذَا سَمِعْتُمُ النِّدَاءَ فَقُوْلُوْا مِثْلَ مَا يَقُوْلُ الْمُؤَذِّنُ

Transliteration:

Idhā sami'tumun-nidā'a Faqūlū mithla mā yaqūlul-mu'adhdhin.(Bukhārī Kitābul-Adhān)

Translation:

Whenever you hear the Adhān, say what the Mu'adhdhin is saying.

Hence, anyone who hears the *Adhān* should repeat the same, phrase by phrase, after the *Mu'adhdhin* has recited them but when the *Mu'adhdhin* says the words *Ḥayya 'alaṣ-Ṣalāh* and *Ḥayya 'alal-Falāḥ,* the person hearing the *Adhān* should say *Lā ḥaula walā quwwata illā billā-hil 'aliyyul 'Aẓīm* which means: *There is neither might nor any power except with Allah.*

If the congregational Prayer is offered in the open, i.e. outside the mosque, even then, *Adhān* should be recited before the Prayer. After completion of the *Adhān*, listeners should recite the following prayer:

اَللّٰهُمَّ رَبَّ هٰذِهِ الدَّعْوَةِ التَّامَّةِ وَالصَّلَاةِ الْقَائِمَةِ آتِ مُحَمَّدَ
ِالْوَسِيْلَةَ وَالْفَضِيْلَةَ وَالدَّرَجَةَ الرَّفِيْعَةَ وَابْعَثْهُ مَقَامًا
مَّحْمُوْدَا ِالَّذِىْ وَعَدْتَّهٗ اِنَّكَ لَا تُخْلِفُ الْمِيْعَادَ

Transliteration:

Allāhumma Rabba hadhihidda'watit-tāmmati waṣṣalātil qā'imati, āti Muḥammada-nil-wasīlata wal-faḍīlata waddarajatar-rafī'ata, wab'ath-hu maqāmam-maḥmūda-nilladhī wa'attahū. Innaka lā tukhliful mī'ād. (Bukhārī, Kitābul-Adhān)

Translation:

O Allah, Lord of this Perfect Call, and of the Congregational Prayer, make Muhammad a means of our access to You, and bless him with excellence and the lofty office, and grant him the most exalted station Thou hast promised him. Verily, Thou goest not back on Thy promise.

IQĀMAT (*IQĀMAH*)

When the Prayer is about to commence, *Iqāmah* is recited. This is an indication that the *Imām* has taken his place facing towards the *Ka'bah* and is ready to begin the Prayer. The *Iqāmah* is a shorter version of the *Adhān*. Other differences between the *Adhān* and the *Iqāmah* are as follows:

i. The *Adhān* is called aloud while the *Iqāmah* is recited in a low tone.

ii. During the recitation of *Iqāmah* the fingers are not raised so as to touch the ears as is done in *Adhān*; instead the arms are left hanging straight by one's sides.

iii. The sentence, *Aṣṣalātu khairum-minan-naum* is not recited in the *Iqāmah*.

iv. The *Iqāmah* is recited rapidly, though the *Mālikī* school of thought recite both the *Iqāmah* as well as the *Adhān*, with pauses between the verses. During the *Iqāmah* the sentence *Qad qāmatiṣ-Ṣalāt,* i.e. *Ṣalāt* is ready, is repeated twice after saying, *Ḥayya 'alal-Falāḥ*.

v. During the *Iqāmah*, the face is not turned towards the right or to the left when *Hayya 'alaṣ-Ṣalāh* and *Ḥayya 'alal-Falāḥ* are recited, as is done in the *Adhān*.

The text of the *Iqāmah* is as follows:

اَللّٰهُ اَكْبَرُ اللّٰهُ اَكْبَرُ، اَشْهَدُ اَنْ لَّا إِلٰهَ إِلَّا اللّٰه، أَشْهَدُ أَنَّ

مُحَمَّدًا رَّسُوْلُ اللّٰهِ، حَيَّ عَلَى الصَّلٰوةِ، حَيَّ عَلَى الْفَلَاحِ، قَدْ
قَامَتِ الصَّلٰوةُ قَدْ قَامَتِ الصَّلٰوةُ، اَللّٰهُ اَكْبَرُ اللّٰهُ اَكْبَرُ، لَا اِلٰهَ
اِلَّا اللّٰهُ۔

Transliteration:

Allāhu Akbar, Allāhu Akbar; Ashhadu allā Ilāha illallāh; Ashhadu anna Muḥammadar Rasūlullāh; Ḥayya 'alaṣ-Ṣalāh; Ḥayya 'alal-Falāḥ; Qad qāmatiṣ-Ṣalātu, Qad qāmatiṣ-ṣalāh; Allāhu Akbar, Allāhu Akbar; Lā Ilāha Illallāh

Translation:

Allah is the Greatest, Allah is Greatest; I bear witness that there is none worthy of worship except Allah; I bear witness that Muhammad is the Messenger of Allah. Come to Prayer. Come to success. Ṣalāt is ready. Allah is the Greatest; Allah is the Greatest; There is none worthy of worship except Allah.

According to the Sayings of the Holy Prophet[sa] the person who has recited the *Adhān* should also recite the *Iqāmah*. (*Sunan Tirmidhī, Abwābuṣ-Ṣalāt, Bāb Mā Jā'a anna man Adhdhana fa huwa yuqīm*). However, in certain cases, another person may recite the *Iqāmah* with the permission of the *Mu'adhdhin* or the *Imām*.

NIYYAT (*NIYYAH*)

Niyyah means the intention to perform a Prayer

and is an essential part of it. The worshipper should make a *Niyyah* in his mind as to which type of Prayer, *Farḍ, Sunnah* or *Nafl* etc., he is going to perform and how many *Rak'āt*. It is not necessary to make *Niyyah* by saying the words aloud. The mere intention in one's mind will suffice. The worshipper, therefore, should recite *Taujīh* along with the *Niyyah*. *Taujīh* is given in chapter 2.

COMBINING PRAYERS

Under certain conditions, two Prayer services may be combined together. For example, *Ẓuhr* Prayer may be combined with *'Aṣr* Prayer. Similarly *Maghrib* Prayer may be combined with *'Ishā'* Prayer, if the following conditions prevail:

a. If a person is sick.
b. If a person is on a journey.
c. During rain or a storm.
d. If it is difficult to go to the mosque because of general discomfort caused by heavy rains.

It is preferable to combine the later Prayer with the earlier Prayer. However, in unavoidable circumstances, the earlier Prayer may be combined with the later one.

When the Prayers are combined, one *Adhān* is sufficient for both Prayers but *Iqāmah* has to be recited separately for each Prayer.

It should also be remembered that the *Sunnat* part of the Prayer service need not be offered when Prayer services are combined together. However, the two

Sunnats performed before the *Jumu'ah* (Friday) Prayer are necessary and should not be omitted.

In case the *Imām* is leading the congregation for *'Aṣr* Prayer and a worshipper who comes late does not know which Prayer is being offered, he should join in anyway. Later, if he comes to know that he has missed the earlier Prayer, he should offer it individually after the congregational Prayer. However, if a worshipper who came in late knows that the *Imām* is leading the later Prayer, he should offer the earlier Prayer individually first and then join in the congregation. For example, if the *Imām* is leading *'Ishā'* Prayer, the latecomer should offer *Maghrib* Prayer, which he has missed, and then join in the congregation. If he does not know that the *Imām* is leading *'Ishā'* Prayer and he joins in thinking that it is *Maghrib* Prayer which the *Imām* is leading, he should carry on following the *Imām*. Afterwards, he has only to offer *Maghrib* Prayer individually, as his *'Ishā'* Prayer behind the *Imām* was valid. In normal circumstances, however, one should offer the earlier Prayer first and the later Prayer afterwards.

CHAPTER TWO

1. THE METHOD OF OFFERING PRAYER

Normally, *Ṣalāt* should be offered in congregation in a mosque, a place dedicated to Divine worship but it may be held anywhere, the only requirement being that the place chosen should be clean.

Before a worshipper commences his Prayer, he should cleanse his body and ensure that his clothes are also clean. He should perform *Wuḍū'* and then stand in a row along with other worshippers behind the *Imām*, the person who leads the Prayer, all facing towards the *Ka'bah*. The rows must be perfectly straight and the worshippers should stand shoulder to shoulder but in no way in a position to interfere with each other's Prayer. The Holy Prophet[sa] was very particular about the straightness of rows.

Thus, arranging themselves in rows behind the *Imām*, each worshipper should then make his intention as to which Prayer he is going to offer and then recite the *Taujīh*. *Taujīh* is as follows:

إِنِّيْ وَجَّهْتُ وَجْهِيَ لِلَّذِيْ فَطَرَ السَّمَاوَاتِ وَالْأَرْضَ حَنِيْفًا

وَّمَا أَنَا مِنَ الْمُشْرِكِيْنَ

Transliteration:

Innī wajjahtu wajhiya lilladhī faṭaras-samāwāti wal arḍa ḥanīfan wamā ana minal mushrikīn.

Translation:

I have turned my full attention towards the Supreme Being, Who has created the heavens and the earth, and I am not one of those who associate partners with Him.

Before the commencement of Prayer, *Iqāmah*, the notice that the Prayer is about to start, is recited.

During the Prayer one should concentrate fully on one's Prayer and remove all other thoughts from one's mind.

The Prayer starts with *Takbīr-i-Taḥrīmah*, i.e. the *Imām* raises both hands to the level of his earlobes and says *Allāhu Akbar* (God is the Greatest). All worshippers do the same. To raise both hands to one's earlobes when reciting *Allāhu Akbar* is to follow the practice (called the *Sunnah*) of the Holy Prophet[sa] of Islam. All Muslim schools of thought agree on this. However, there are some Muslim sects who raise their hands to their earlobes more than once in one *Rak'at*. Thus, in addition to the moment of saying the first *Allāhu Akbar* at the start of Prayer, they also raise their hands while going to *Rukū'* posture from Standing; when reverting to the standing posture; when going to *Sajdah* and when getting up from *Sajdah*. Looking at the history of Islam, we find that the Holy Prophet[sa] did raise his hands more than once during Prayer on several occasions in the early days of his ministry as mentioned in the books of Traditions but this was not his common practice. According to many other Sayings of the Holy Prophet[sa] of Islam he never raised his hands except when saying *Takbīr-i-Taḥrīmah* in the first *Rak'at* of every Prayer. A Companion of the Holy Prophet[sa] Ḥaḍrat 'Abdullāh ibn Mas'ūd[ra] is reported to have stated:

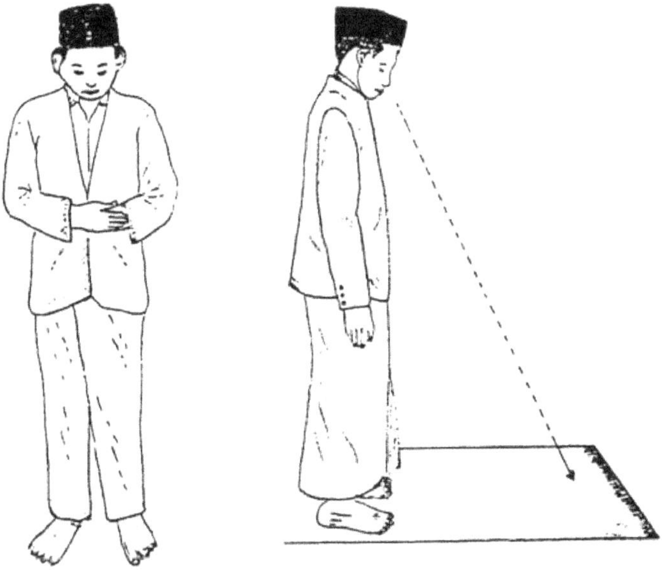

Let me show you how the Holy Prophet[sa] of Islam used to offer his Prayer. 'Abdullāh then offered his Prayer and raised his hands only in the beginning when saying Takbīr-i-Taḥrīmah.

After raising his hands to the lobes of his ears and reciting *Allāhu Akbar*, the *Imām* lowers his hands and folds them on his chest so that the right arm is over his left arm. The worshipper stands before his Lord, an attitude of utmost humility. His hands folded on his chest most respectfully is called the *Qiyām*, the

Standing Posture. However, there are variations in this posture. Some people fold their arms a little lower than the navel while others slightly above the navel and some even a little higher. These are all signs of respect. One should not be so petty minded as to quarrel with others regarding these minor matters. It should also be noted that generally, the *Mālikī* among the *Sunnis* and the *Shia* do not fold their arms at all. They leave them straight by their sides. Though no Hadith is available to prove that the Holy Prophet[sa] ever did so, yet no one has the right to object and say that the Prayers of such people who do not fold their arms are not valid. After saying *Takbīr-i-Taḥrīmah*, the following glorification called *Thanā'* is recited individually in silence:

سُبْحَانَكَ اللّٰهُمَّ وَبِحَمْدِكَ وَتَبَارَكَ اسْمُكَ وَتَعَالٰى جَدُّكَ

وَلَا إِلٰهَ غَيْرُكَ

Transliteration:

Subḥānakallāh-humma wa biḥamdika wa tabārakasmuka wa ta'ālā jadduka walā ilāha ghairuk.

Translation:

Holy art Thou, O Allah, and all praise is Thine; blessed is Thy name, and exalted is Thy state. There is none worthy of worship except Thee alone. (Tirmidhī, Kitābuṣ-Ṣalāt, Mā Yaqūlu inda iftāhiṣ-Ṣalāti; Sunan Nasa'ī, Kitābul-Iftāh, Bābudh-Dhikr bainaṣ-Ṣalāt wa bainal-Qirā'at.)

It is also reported in some Sayings that sometimes, the Holy Prophet[sa] of Islam used to recite other verses in place of this glorification but this is the one which is well-known and often recited. The above glorification is followed by *Ta'awwudh*, which is also recited silently:

اَعُوْذُ بِاللّٰهِ مِنَ الشَّيْطَانِ الرَّجِيْمِ

Transliteration:

A'ūdhu billāhi minash-shaiṭānir-rajīm.

Translation:

I seek refuge with Allah from Satan, the accursed.

After *Ta'awwudh, Bismillāh* is recited either silently or loudly, by the *Imām*. The congregation, however, recites it silently. *Tasmiyah* is as follows:

بِسْمِ اللّٰهِ الرَّحْمٰنِ الرَّحِيْمِ

Transliteration:

Bismillāhir-Raḥmānir-Raḥīm.

Translation:

In the name of Allah, the Gracious, the Merciful.

According to the Traditions, on some occasions, the Holy Prophet[sa] used to say *Tasmiyah* aloud while on other occasions he recited it silently. Among Muslims, it is generally recited aloud in Arab countries while the *Ḥanafī* sect and a large number of other Muslims recite it silently.

The *Imām* then recites *Sūrah Al-Fātiḥah*. In certain Prayers, e.g., *Fajr*, *Maghrib* and *'Ishā'* Prayers, he recites it loudly, while in others, *Ẓuhr* and *'Aṣr* he and other worshippers, following him, recite it silently. When the *Imām* is reciting *Sūrah Al-Fātiḥah* loudly, the other worshippers should repeat it silently, verse by verse, during the short interval between the verses after the *Imām* has recited those verses.

بِسْمِ اللّٰهِ الرَّحْمٰنِ الرَّحِيْمِ ۝ اَلْحَمْدُ لِلّٰهِ رَبِّ الْعٰلَمِيْنَ ۝
الرَّحْمٰنِ الرَّحِيْمِ ۝ مٰلِكِ يَوْمِ الدِّيْنِ ۝ اِيَّاكَ نَعْبُدُ وَ اِيَّاكَ
نَسْتَعِيْنُ ۝ اِهْدِنَا الصِّرَاطَ الْمُسْتَقِيْمَ ۝ صِرَاطَ الَّذِيْنَ
اَنْعَمْتَ عَلَيْهِمْ ۙ غَيْرِ الْمَغْضُوْبِ عَلَيْهِمْ وَلَا الضَّآلِّيْنَ ۝

Transliteration:

Bismillāhir-Raḥmānir-Raḥīm. Al-ḥamdu lillāhi Rabbil 'ālamīn. Ar-raḥmānir-Raḥīm. Māliki yaumiddīn. Iyyāka na'budu wa iyyāka nasta'īn. Ihdinaṣ-ṣirāt al-mustaqīm. Ṣirātalladhīna an'amta 'alai-him, ghairil maghḍūbi 'alaihim wa laḍ-ḍāllīn.

Translation:

In the name of Allah, the Gracious, the Merciful. All praise belongs to Allah, Lord of all the worlds, The Gracious, the Merciful, Master of the Day of Judgment. Thee alone do we worship and Thee alone do we implore for help. Guide us in the right path—The path of those on whom Thou hast bestowed Thy blessings, those who have not incurred Thy displeasure, and those who have not gone astray.

At the end of *Sūrah Al-Fātiḥah*, the worshippers say *Āmīn* which means 'O Allah! Accept our supplications.'

The members of the *Mālikī*, *Shāf'ī* and *Ḥanbalī* sects of Islam say *Āmīn* loudly while the members of the *Ḥanafī* sect say it silently. Both forms are admissible. This is not one of those matters which makes *Ṣalāt* valid or invalid. One can adopt whatever method one likes, i.e. to say it aloud or to say it silently. No one else should have the right to object, except when someone says it so loudly that other worshippers are disturbed. Thereafter, the *Imām* recites a portion of the Holy Quran, at least three verses or a short chapter. For example:

SŪRAH AL-KAUTHAR

بِسْمِ اللّٰهِ الرَّحْمٰنِ الرَّحِيْمِ ○ اِنَّآ اَعْطَيْنٰكَ الْكَوْثَرَ ○ فَصَلِّ
لِرَبِّكَ وَانْحَرْ ○ اِنَّ شَانِئَكَ هُوَ الْاَبْتَرُ ○

Transliteration:

Bismillāhir-Raḥmānir-Raḥīm. Innā a'aṭainākal-Kauthar. Faṣalli lirabbika wanḥar. Inna shāni'aka huwal abtar.

Translation:

In the name of Allah, the Gracious, the Merciful. Surely We have given thee abundance of good; So pray to thy Lord, and offer sacrifice. Surely, it is thy enemy who is without issue.

SŪRAH AL-IKHLĀṢ

بِسۡمِ اللّٰہِ الرَّحۡمٰنِ الرَّحِیۡمِ ۝ قُلۡ ہُوَ اللّٰہُ اَحَدٌ ۝ اَللّٰہُ
الصَّمَدُ ۝ لَمۡ یَلِدۡ ۬ۙ وَ لَمۡ یُوۡلَدۡ ۝ وَ لَمۡ یَکُنۡ لَّہٗ کُفُوًا اَحَدٌ ۝

Transliteration:

Bismillāhir-Raḥmānir-Raḥīm. Qul huwallāhu Aḥad. Allāhuṣ-Ṣamad. Lam yalid, walam yūlad. Walam yakullahū kufuwan aḥad.

Translation:

In the name of Allah, the Gracious, the Merciful. Say, He is Allah, the One; Allah, the Independent and Besought of all. He begets not, nor is He begotten; And there is none like unto Him.

SŪRAH AL-FALAQ

بِسۡمِ اللّٰہِ الرَّحۡمٰنِ الرَّحِیۡمِ ۝ قُلۡ اَعُوۡذُ بِرَبِّ الۡفَلَقِ ۝ مِنۡ
شَرِّ مَا خَلَقَ ۝ وَ مِنۡ شَرِّ غَاسِقٍ اِذَا وَقَبَ ۝ وَ مِنۡ شَرِّ النَّفّٰثٰتِ
فِی الۡعُقَدِ ۝ وَ مِنۡ شَرِّ حَاسِدٍ اِذَا حَسَدَ ۝

Transliteration:

Bismillāhir-Raḥmānir-Raḥīm. Qul a'ūdhu birabbil falaq. Min sharri mā khalaq. Wa min sharri ghāsiqin idhā waqab. Wa min sharrin-naffāthāti fil-'uqad. Wa min sharri ḥāsidin idhā ḥasad.

Translation:

In the name of Allah, the Gracious, the Merciful. Say, I seek refuge in the Lord of the dawn, From the evil of that which He has created, And from the evil of the night when it overspreads, And from the evil of those who blow into knots to undo them, And from the evil of the envier when he envies.

SŪRAH AN-NĀS

بِسْمِ اللّٰهِ الرَّحْمٰنِ الرَّحِيْمِ ۝ قُلْ اَعُوْذُ بِرَبِّ النَّاسِ ۝

مَلِكِ النَّاسِ ۝ اِلٰهِ النَّاسِ ۝ مِنْ شَرِّ الْوَسْوَاسِ الْخَنَّاسِ ۝

الَّذِيْ يُوَسْوِسُ فِيْ صُدُوْرِ النَّاسِ ۝ مِنَ الْجِنَّةِ وَالنَّاسِ ۝

Transliteration:

Bismillāhir-Raḥmānir-Raḥīm. Qul a'ūdhu birabbin-nās, Mālikin-nās, Ilāhin-nās, Min sharril waswāsil khannās. Alladhī yuwaswisu fī ṣudūrin-nās, minal jinnati wan-nās.

Translation:

In the name of Allah, the Gracious, the Merciful. Say, I seek refuge in the Lord of mankind, The King of mankind, The God of mankind, From the evil of the sneaking whisperer, Who whispers into the hearts of men, From among the Jinn and mankind.

These few *Sūrahs* of the Quran which we have stated above are only a sample. The *Imām* may choose any portion of the Quran to recite after the *Sūrah Al-Fātiḥah*.

When the *Imām* is reciting a portion of the Holy Quran, the worshippers are required to listen to it silently. The Holy Quran says:

وَ اِذَا قُرِئَ الْقُرْاٰنُ فَاسْتَمِعُوْا لَهٗ وَ اَنْصِتُوْا لَعَلَّكُمْ تُرْحَمُوْنَ۝

Translation:

And when the Quran is recited, give ear to it and keep silence, that you may be shown mercy. (7:205)

A Companion of the Holy Prophet[sa] Ḥaḍrat 'Ibādah ibn Ṣāmit[ra], relates that once the Holy Prophet[sa] while leading the *Fajr* Prayer, found it too difficult to recite the verses of the Quran because of the murmur at the back. When he finished his Prayer, the Holy Prophet[sa] asked his Companions whether they were reciting the verses of the Quran after him. Their reply was in the affirmative at which the Holy Prophet[sa] said:

Do not recite the verses of the Quran after the Imām, except the recitation of Sūrah Al-Fātiḥah as Sūrah Al-Fātiḥah is an integral part of the Ṣalāt.

It is essential that every member of the congregation takes care not to cause disturbance to other worshippers and therefore Muslims should take note of the above mentioned Hadith of the Holy Prophet[sa] of Islam.

At the end of the recitation, the *Imām* goes from

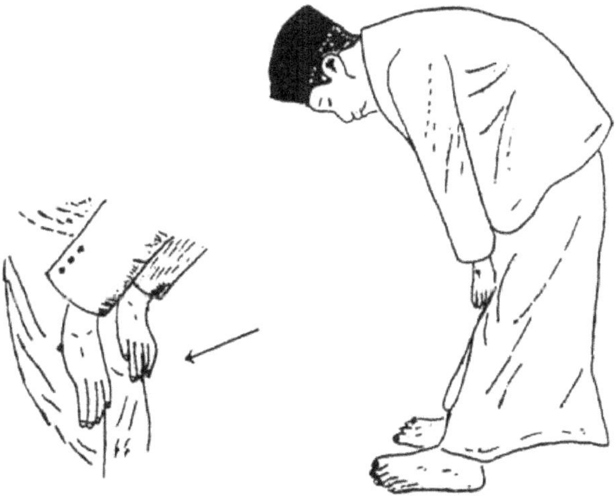

the Standing position to the Bowing position, *Rukū'*, by calling out *Allāhu Akbar*. The other worshippers follow him into the Bowing position. In this posture, the right hand of the worshipper should press the right knee and the left hand the left knee, and the upper half of the body from the waist to the head is kept level and horizontal to the ground.

In the Bowing posture the following *Tasbīḥ* is recited silently three times or more in odd numbers:

سُبْحَانَ رَبِّيَ الْعَظِيْمُ

Transliteration:
Subḥāna Rabbiyal 'Aẓīm.

Translation:

Holy is my Lord, the Most Great.

The *Imām* then straightens up and stands with his arms by his sides. When he initiates this movement, he recites *Tasmī'* loudly which is an indication for the congregation to change the posture from Bowing to Standing.
The *Tasmī'* is recited as follows:

سَمِعَ اللّٰهُ لِمَنْ حَمِدَهٗ

Transliteration:
Sami'allāhu liman ḥamidah

Translation:

Allah listens to him who praises Him.

In response the congregation follows the *Imām* and changes posture as well, and then recite the following which is called *Taḥmīd:*

رَبَّنَا وَلَكَ الْحَمْدُ حَمْدًا كَثِيرًا طَيِّبًا مُبَارَكًا فِيْهِ

Transliteration:

Rabbanā walakal-ḥamd, ḥamdan kathīran Ṭayyiban Mubārakan fīh.

Translation:

Our Lord, Thine is the praise, the praise which is bountiful, pure and blessed.

This position of standing erect ends with the recitation of *Taḥmīd*.

Then the *Imām* says *Allāhu Akbar* loudly again and leads the congregation into the Prostration position called *Sajdah,* knees on the ground, then the head. In this posture, the knees, hands, nose and the

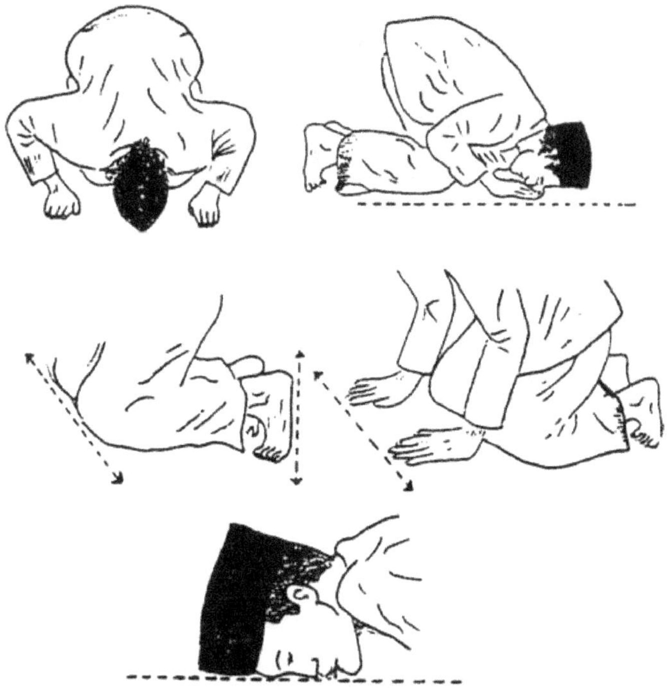

forehead of the worshipper should be touching the ground. The head should be placed on the ground between the two hands. The arms should be away from the ground and away from one's sides. The Holy Prophet[sa] has said:

When you prostrate before God, you should place your limbs on the ground in the correct manner. In no way should you spread your arms on the ground like the front legs of a dog when it sits. (Musnad Aḥmad bin Ḥanbal, vol. III, p.279; Al-Maktabah-Islāmī, Ṭab'a wan-Nashr, Beirut..)

The fingers are held together pointing towards the *Ka'bah*. The feet should be planted on the ground so that the toes are bent in the direction of the *Ka'bah*.

In this posture the *Tasbīḥ* given below should be recited silently three times at least. If the worshipper wishes to recite it more than three times, he should make sure that the number of recitations are odd and not even:

سُبْحَانَ رَبِّيَ الْأَعْلٰى

Transliteration:

Subḥāna Rabbiyal-a'lā.

Translation:

Glory to my Lord, the Most High.

Prostration is a posture of utmost humility, submission and helplessness in which a supplicant pours his heart before God Almighty and asks for His forgiveness.

It should also be noted that during the *Rukū'* and *Sajdah*, the Holy Prophet[sa] has forbidden the recitation of any Quranic verse. *(Ṣaḥīḥ Muslim, Kitābuṣ-Ṣalāt, Bābun Manāhī an Qira'til-Quran fir-rukū' was-sujūd.)*

The *Imām* then says *Allāhu Akbar* again, at which he and the congregation raise their heads and then their hands from the ground and go into the Sitting position called *Jilsah*. When sitting in this position, the worshipper spreads his left foot horizontally on the ground and rests on it while his right foot is placed on the ground in a perpendicular position, with the toes facing the *Ka'bah*. The hands are placed on the thighs with the fingers pointing towards the *Ka'bah*, very close to the knees. In this position, the following supplication is recited silently:

اَللّٰهُمَّ اغْفِرْ لِيْ، وَارْحَمْنِي، وَاهْدِنِيْ، وَعَافِنِيْ، وَارْفَعْنِيْ وَ

اجْبُرْنِيْ، وَارْزُقْنِيْ

Transliteration:

Allāhum-maghfir lī warḥamnī wahdinī wa 'āfinī warfa'nī wajburnī warzuqnī.

Translation:

Lord forgive me and have mercy on me and guide me and grant me security and raise me up and make good my shortcomings and provide for me.

After *Jilsah*, the *Imām* leads the congregation into a second Prostration by saying *Allāhu Akbar* and, again *Subḥāna Rabbiyal A'lā* is done three times or, if more, in odd number. In every *Rak'at* of Prayer there are always two Prostrations. At the end of the second prostration, one *Rak'at* of Prayer is completed. After saying *Allāhu Akbar* once again, the *Imām* leads the congregation into the Standing posture to commence the second *Rak'at* which is offered exactly as the first *Rak'at*.

However, during the second *Rak'at*, *Thanā'* (Glorification) and *Ta'awwudh* are not recited. *Thanā'* and *Ta'awwudh* are recited only in the first *Rak'at* of every Prayer. The *Imām* recites *Sūrah Al-Fātiḥah* and then some verses of the Holy Quran and completes the *Rak'at* in the same manner as the first. After the second Prostration, he sits down in the same manner as he sat in the position called *Jilsah*. This Sitting Position, at the end of the second *Rak'at* is called *Qa'dah*. During this position *Tashahhud* is recited silently, which is as follows:

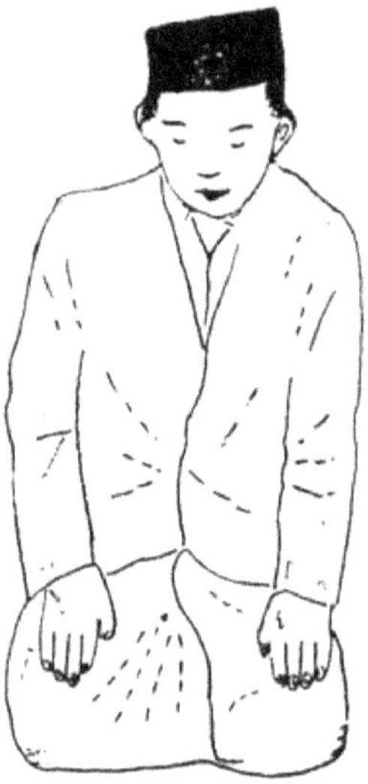

اَلتَّحِيَّاتُ لِلّٰهِ وَالصَّلَوَاتُ وَالطَّيِّبَاتُ، اَلسَّلَامُ عَلَيْكَ أَيُّهَا

النَّبِيُّ وَرَحْمَةُ اللّٰهِ وَبَرَكَاتُهٗ. اَلسَّلَامُ عَلَيْنَا وَعَلٰى عِبَادِ اللّٰهِ الصَّالِحِيْنَ. أَشْهَدُ أَنْ لَّا إِلٰهَ إِلَّا اللّٰهُ وَأَشْهَدُ أَنَّ مُحَمَّدًا عَبْدُهٗ وَرَسُوْلُهٗ

Transliteration:

Attaḥiyyātu lillāhi waṣ-ṣalawātu waṭ-ṭayyibātu, Assalāmu 'alaika ayyuhan-Nabiyyu wa Raḥmatullāhi wa Barakātuh, Assalāmu 'alainā wa 'alā ibādillāhiṣ-Ṣaliḥīn. Ashhadu allā ilāha illallāhu wa ashhadu anna Muḥammadan 'abduhū wa Rasūluh.

Translation:

All Salutation is due to Allah and all Prayer and everything pure. Peace be upon thee, O Prophet, and the mercy of Allah and His blessings; and peace be on us and on all righteous servants of Allah. I bear witness that there is none worthy of worship except Allah, and I bear witness that Muhammad is His servant and Messenger.

It should be noted that while reciting *Tashahhud*, when the worshipper reaches the phrase *Ashhadu allā ilāha illallāhu*, he should raise the forefinger of his right hand and should drop it down as he has recited it. It is written in the Books of Traditions that the Holy Prophet[sa] used to close the fingers of his right hand leaving the thumb and the forefinger free, placing the hand on the right knee and raising the forefinger while reciting *Ashhadu allā ilāha illallāhu* and dropping it to its original position as soon as he had recited it. The fingers of the left hand would remain straight on his left knee.

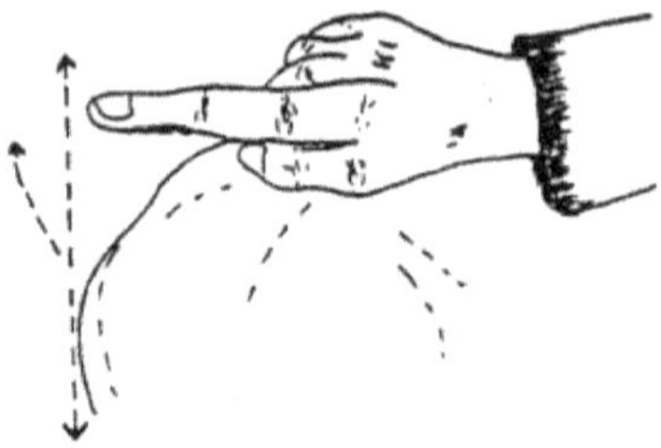

After reciting *Tashahhud*, the invocation of blessings on the Holy Prophet[sa] called *Durūd (Aṣṣalātu-'alan-nabī)* and some other prayers are recited silently.

DURŪD (*AṢṢALĀTU 'ALAN-NABĪ*)

اَللّٰهُمَّ صَلِّ عَلٰى مُحَمَّدٍ وَّعَلٰى آلِ مُحَمَّدٍ كَمَا صَلَّيْتَ عَلٰى
إِبْرَاهِيْمَ وَعَلٰى آلِ إِبْرَاهِيْمَ إِنَّكَ حَمِيْدٌ مَّجِيْدٌ. اَللّٰهُمَّ بَارِكْ
عَلٰى مُحَمَّدٍ وَّعَلٰى آلِ مُحَمَّدٍ كَمَا بَارَكْتَ عَلٰى إِبْرَاهِيْمَ وَعَلٰى آلِ
إِبْرَاهِيْمَ إِنَّكَ حَمِيْدٌ مَّجِيْدٌ۔

Transliteration:

Allāhumma ṣalli 'alā Muḥammadin wa 'alā āli Muḥammadin kamā ṣallaita 'alā Ibrāhīma wa 'alā āli Ibrāhīma innaka Ḥamīdum-Majīd. Allāhumma Bārik 'alā Muḥammadin wa 'alā āli Muḥammadin kamā Bārakta 'alā Ibrāhīma wa 'alā āli Ibrāhīma innaka Ḥamīdum-Majīd.

Translation:

Bless, O Allah, Muhammad and the people of Muhammad, as Thou didst bless Abraham and the people of Abraham. Thou art indeed the Praiseworthy, the Glorious. Prosper, O Allah, Muhammad and the people of Muhammad, as Thou didst prosper Abraham and the people of Abraham. Thou are the Praiseworthy, the Glorious.

The invocation *Durūd (Aṣṣalātu 'alan-nabī)* is followed by a short prayer or prayers, some of which are given below:

رَبَّنَآ اٰتِنَا فِي الدُّنْيَا حَسَنَةً وَّ فِي الْاٰخِرَةِ حَسَنَةً وَّ قِنَا عَذَابَ النَّارِ○

Transliteration:

Rabbanā ātinā fiddunyā ḥasanatan wa fil ākhirati ḥasanatan waqinā adhābannār. (2:202)

Translation:

Our Lord, grant us good in this world as well as good in the world to come, and protect us from the torment of the Fire.

رَبِّ اجْعَلْنِيْ مُقِيْمَ الصَّلٰوةِ وَ مِنْ ذُرِّيَّتِيْ رَبَّنَا وَ تَقَبَّلْ دُعَآءِ○

رَبَّنَا اغْفِرْ لِيْ وَلِوَالِدَيَّ وَلِلْمُؤْمِنِيْنَ يَوْمَ يَقُوْمُ الْحِسَابُ

Transliteration:

Rabbij'alnī muqīmaṣ-Ṣalāti wamin dhur-riyyatī. Rabbanā wa taqabbal du'ā'. Rabbanaghfir lī wali-wālidayya wa lil-mu'minīna yauma yaqūmul ḥisāb. (14:41-42)

Translation:

My Lord, make me observe Prayer, and my children too. Our Lord! bestow Thy grace on me and accept my prayer. Our Lord, grant forgiveness to me and to my parents and to the believers on the day when the reckoning will take place.

اَللّٰهُمَّ اِنِّيْ اَعُوْذُبِكَ مِنَ الْهَمِّ وَالْحُزْنِ وَاَعُوْذُبِكَ مِنَ الْعَجْزِ وَالْكَسْلِ وَاَعُوْذُبِكَ مِنَ الْجُبْنِ وَالْبُخْلِ وَاَعُوْذُبِكَ مِنْ غَلْبَةِ الدَّيْنِ وَقَهْرِ الرِّجَالِ

Transliteration:

'Allāhumma innī a'ūdhu bika minal-hammi wal-ḥuzni, wa a'ūdhu bika minal 'ajzi wal kasli, wa a'ūdhu bika minal jubni wal-bukhli. Wa a'ūdhu bika min ghalbatid-daini wa qahrir-rijāl. (Sunan Abū Dāwūd, Kitābuṣ-Ṣalāt).

Translation:

O Allah, I seek Thy protection against problems and

anxieties, and I seek Thy protection against helplessness and shiftlessness, and I seek Thy protection against cowardice and miserliness, and I seek Thy protection against indebtedness and the tyranny of people.

اَللّٰهُمَّ إِنِّي ظَلَمْتُ نَفْسِي ظُلْمًا كَثِيرًا، وَلَا يَغْفِرُ الذُّنُوبَ إِلَّا أَنْتَ۔ فَاغْفِرْ لِي مَغْفِرَةً مِّنْ عِنْدِكَ، وَارْحَمْنِي إِنَّكَ أَنْتَ الْغَفُوْرُ الرَّحِيْمُ۔

Transliteration:

Allāhumma innī ẓalamtu nafsī ẓulman kathīran, wa lā yaghfirudh-dhunūba illā anta, faghfir lī maghfiratan min ʻindika warḥamnī innaka antal Ghafūrur-Raḥīm.

Translation:

O Allah, I have been unjust to myself and no one grants pardon for sins except You; therefore, forgive me with Your forgiveness and have mercy on me. Surely You are the Forgiver, the Merciful.

اَللّٰهُمَّ إِنِّي أَعُوْذُ بِكَ مِنْ عَذَابِ الْقَبْرِ، وَأَعُوْذُ بِكَ مِنْ فِتْنَةِ الْمَسِيحِ الدَّجَّالِ، وَأَعُوْذُ بِكَ مِنْ فِتْنَةِ الْمَحْيَا وَالْمَمَاتِ۔

اَللّٰهُمَّ إِنِّي أَعُوْذُ بِكَ مِنَ الْمَأْثَمِ وَالْمَغْرَمِ

Transliteration:

Allāhumma innī a'ūdhu bika min 'adhābil-qabri wa a'ūdhu bika min fitnatil-masīḥid-dajjāl. Wa a'ūdhu bika min fitnatil maḥyā wal mamāt. Allāhumma innī a'ūdhu bika minal ma'thami wal maghram.

Translation:

O Allah, I seek Thy protection from the punishment of the grave, and I seek Thy protection against Dajjāl, the architect of disorder and trials, and I seek refuge with You from afflictions of life and death. O Allah, I seek Thy protection from sins and from being in debt.

After reciting one or more of these prayers, the *Imām* turns his face towards the right and says *Assalāmu 'Alaikum wa Raḥmatullāh,* i.e. peace be upon you and the mercy of Allah, and then turns his face towards the left and repeats *Assalāmu 'Alaikum wa Raḥmatullāh*, to mark the end of the Prayer. The

congregation does the same. If the Prayer which is being performed is not of two *Rak'āt* but is a three or four *Rak'āt* Prayer, then sitting in the *Qa'dah* position at the end of the second *Rak'at*, is shortened and the worshipper recites only up to and including *Tashahhud.* Having recited *Tashahhud*, the *Imām* says *Allāhu Akbar* indicating the end of the second *Rak'at* and the beginning of the third *Rak'at*, and assumes the *Qiyām* posture, completes the third *Rak'at* exactly as he has done the second. The whole congregation follows him. If the Prayer is of three *Rak'āt*, for example *Maghrib* Prayer, then after the second prostration of the third *Rak'at*, the *Imām* sits in the *Qa'dah* position, recites *Tashahhud* and *Durūd* and some other prayers silently and says *Assalāmu 'Alaikum wa Raḥmatullāh*, marking the end of the Prayer. The whole congregation follows his movements and recite the same silently.

If the Prayer is a four *Rak'āt* Prayer, like *Ẓuhr, 'Aṣr* and *'Ishā'*, the *Imām* does not assume the *Qa'dah* posture at the end of the third *Rak'at*, but leads the congregation immediately into the *Qiyām* of the fourth *Rak'at.* It is only after the second Prostration of the fourth *Rak'at* that the *Imām* sits in the *Qa'dah* position. In this *Qa'dah* which is called final *Qa'dah*, recite *Durūd* and prayers after *Tashahhud*. They then end the Prayer by saying *Assalāmu 'Alaikum wa Raḥmatullāh* while turning their face towards the right and to the left as explained earlier. The following points should be noted:

i. If it is the final *Qa'dah*, *Tashahhud* and *Durūd* and

some other prayers are recited. If it is not the final *Qa'dah*, only *Tashahhud* is recited and after saying *Allāhu Akbar* the next *Rak'at* is started.

ii. If the Prayer being performed is a two *Rak'āt* Prayer, the *Qa'dah* after the second *Rak'at* is the final *Qa'dah*.

iii. If it is a three *Rak'āt* Prayer, the *Qa'dah* at the end of the third *Rak'at* is the final *Qa'dah*.

iv. If it is a four *Rak'āt* Prayer the *Qa'dah* at the end of the fourth *Rak'at* is the final *Qa'dah*.

INDIVIDUAL PRAYER

Even if Prayer is not offered in congregation but offered individually, it is offered exactly in the same way as when led by an *Imām*, except that whatever the *Imām* recites loudly, is not recited loudly by the individual worshipper. He recites everything silently, without raising his voice. For example, when he recites *Sūrah Al-Fātiḥah*, or says *Allāhu Akbar*, *Sami'allāhu liman Ḥamidah* and *Assalāmu 'Alaikum*, he recites all of these silently.

CONGREGATIONAL PRAYER

Every Muslim is required to offer the *Farḍ* part of his Prayers in congregation. Mosques are built for the purpose of congregational Prayers. A Hadith tells us that the reward of a Prayer offered in congregation is twenty-seven times more than that offered individually.

The *Imām* should be chosen by the congregation, keeping in mind that to the best of their knowledge, he is a pious person and the most well-versed among them in the Holy Quran. The *Imām* can also be appointed if there is a regular religious authority, e.g., a *Khalīfah*. Whoever is chosen or appointed as *Imām* must be followed in the Prayer even if somebody thinks that the appointed person is not worthy of it. For those people who doubt the worthiness of an *Imām*, the following instructions of the Holy Prophet[sa] should suffice:

عَنْ اَبِيْ هُرَيْرَةَ قَالَ قَالَ رَسُولُ اللّٰهِ صَلَّى اللّٰهُ عَلَيْهِ وَسَلَّمَ

اَلصَّلٰوةُ الْمَكْتُوبَةُ وَاجِبَةٌ خَلْفَ كُلِّ مُسْلِمٍ، بَارًّا كَانَ اَوْ

فَاجِرًا وَإِنْ عَمِلَ الْكَبَائِرَ۔

Transliteration:

'An Abī Hurairah qāla Qāla Rasūlullāhi ṣallallāhu 'alaihi wa sallam: Aṣṣalātul maktūbatu Wājibatun khalfa kulli Muslimin, bārran kāna au fājiran wa in 'amilal kabā'ir. (*Sunan Abū Dawūd, aljuz'ul-awwal, Kitābuṣ-Ṣalāt*)

Translation:

Ḥaḍrat Abū Hurairah[ra] related that the Holy Prophet[sa] stated: To offer Farḍ Prayer behind any Muslim Imām is essential, whether he is a pious person or a sinner, even if he had committed a grievous sin.

If, at the prescribed time for any Prayer, two or

more men are present away from a mosque, they are required to observe the prayer in congregation. When only two males come together for Prayers, one of them should lead the Prayer. They should stand together so that the 2nd person stands on the right side of the *Imām*.

If a man performs his Prayer at home and a female member of the family like to join him, then, she should stand on his left. In the case where two men are already offering their prayer in congregation, and worshippers arrive, they should arrange themselves in a row so that the *Imām* remains in the middle. In normal cases when three or more persons offer their prayer in congregation, the *Imām* should stand in front, all facing towards the *Ka'bah*. In exceptional cases however, the *Imām* can also stand in the middle of the first row along with other worshippers.

According to some schools of thought, there should be at least two persons in the last row behind the *Imām*. These schools of jurisprudence even permit gently pulling someone from the last row so as to form a new row with two persons instead of one.

Other schools discourage this act, as it not only causes disturbance to the person who is gently pulled but also to the others who are already engaged in prayer.

2. SOME OTHER POINTS TO BE REMEMBERED

1. The worshippers in the front row are rewarded more than the worshippers in the back row,

according to a Saying of the Holy Prophet[sa]. The reason is that those who come early, continue remembering God Almighty while they wait for the Prayer to commence; naturally they are in communion with Allah during more time as compared to the people who come later.

Again, the Holy Prophet[sa] instructed that a new row should not be started until the previous one is fully filled. It is therefore clear that those who come early and occupy the first row and spend more time in the remembrance of God Almighty will be rewarded more than those who come just in time while the *Takbīr* is being recited or even later. These are the people who occupy the back rows.

2. If the Prayer has already started, the latecomer should join in the congregation in the position in which he finds them. For example, if they are in the Standing position, he should start his Prayer in standing position but if they are prostrating, he should join the congregation in prostration.

   When the *Imām* ends the congregational Prayer by saying the Salutation, i.e. *Assalāmu 'Alaikum wa Raḥmatullāh* and turning his face towards the right and towards the left, the person who joined the Prayer later should go into *Qiyām* position and complete the remaining *Rak'āt* of his Prayer individually.

3. *Ṣalāt* consists of units. Each unit is called a *Rak'at*. There are two *Rak'āt* and four *Rak'āt* Prayers in the *Farḍ* of obligatory Prayer.

   Each unit or *Rak'at* consists of the following

essential component parts:

i. The posture of standing called *Qiyām*.

ii. The posture of Bowing down with the hands on one's knees called *Rukū'*.

iii. The position of Standing erect again with arms on the sides called *Qaumah*.

iv. The position of Prostration called *Sajdah*. There are two Prostrations in one *Rak'at*.

v. *Jilsah*: The position of sitting in between the two Prostrations.

vii. *Qa'dah*: The position of sitting after the two Prostrations. If a latecomer joins the congregation before or during the *Rukū'*, then it is deemed that he had offered that *Rak'at* and he does not have to offer it again at the end of the Prayer. If he misses both the initial Standing position (*Qiyām*) and the Bowing position (*Rukū'*) and joins later in that *Rak'at* he has to offer the whole *Rak'at* again at the end of the Prayer when the *Imām* has done both salutations.

4. Once the congregational Prayer has begun, one should not commence with *Sunnat* and *Nafl* Prayer. If someone is already engaged in *Sunnat* Prayer when the *Imām* starts the Prayer, and he finds himself in the middle of a row formed for the congregational Prayer, he should terminate his Prayer immediately and join in the congregation. If he is offering his *Sunnat* or *Nafl* Prayer away from the Prayer Service and he thinks that he can join in the congregation without losing much of the first

Rak'at, he may complete his Prayer; otherwise he should terminate his Prayer and join in the congregation.

5. If the Prayer has already started, it is forbidden for a worshipper to run and join in the congregation.

6. Out of respect for their chastity and honour, women are not advised to stand for Prayer in front of men. For this reason, the rows of women are always behind the men's rows. This gives the women complete freedom to offer their Prayers in the back rows without being embarrassed by the presence of men. It is preferable however, to have a separate enclosure for women. It also follows from the above that a woman cannot lead a congregation of men, but can lead a congregation of women. This means that she can lead a congregation consisting of children of either sex among the worshippers, but not adult men.

7. Women need not say *Adhān* for their congregational Prayers. The female *Imām* stands in the middle of the first row, according to common practice, and not ahead of the congregation as in the case of a male *Imām*.

8. If the *Imām* commits a mistake while leading the congregation, the following method is adopted to point it out to him:

i. If the mistake is an incorrect recitation of the Holy Quran, or the *Imām* has forgotten a verse of the Holy Quran, anyone in the congregation who clearly remembers the correct wording, should remind the *Imām* by reciting the correct verse in a clear and audible voice.

ii. If the *Imām* commits any other mistake, a member of the congregation should draw his attention to it by saying *Subḥānallāh. Subḥānallāh* means 'Allah is free from all faults.' It gives a cue to the *Imām* that he may have committed a mistake. If so, the *Imām* should rectify his mistake. If he does not correct his error, the congregation has to follow him and no one has the right to differ with him during the Prayer. They must follow the *Imām* even in his mistake. However, he should be told of his mistake after the Prayer. Then he should lead the congregation to two additional Prostrations by way of condoning the mistake before turning his face to right and left and again repeating *Assalāmu 'Alaikum wa Raḥmatullāh.* These are called *Sujūd-us-Sahv* or the Prostrations of condonement.

9. If a woman wants to draw the attention of the *Imām* to a mistake which he had committed, she is not allowed to say *Subḥānallāh* aloud; instead, she should clap her hands. The sound of clapping from women conveys to the *Imām* the message that he has committed a mistake. In the case where a female *Imām* commits a mistake during Prayer, her followers may draw her attention to it by either reciting the verse correctly or by saying *Subḥānallāh*, as the case may be.

10. The *Imām* should not prolong the

congregational Prayer to the extent that the worshippers who are praying with him get tired. He should keep in mind that there might be people of old age or who are sick or weak in the congregation and also people who have to attend to other duties after the Prayer.

3. REMEMBRANCE OF ALLAH AFTER CONCLUSION OF THE PRAYER

Continuing the remembrance of Allah for a little while when the *Ṣalāt* is over and engaging in *Tasbīḥ* and *Taḥmīd* follows from the explicit injunction of the Holy Quran. Allah says in Chapter 4, verse 104:

فَإِذَا قَضَيْتُمُ الصَّلٰوةَ فَاذْكُرُوا اللّٰهَ

Transliteration:

Fa idhā qaḍaitumuṣ-Ṣalāta fadhkurullāh.

Translation:

And when you have finished the Prayer, remember Allah.

It is also established by the practice of the Holy Prophet[sa] of Islam. Ḥaḍrat 'Ā'ishah[ra] relates that after finishing his Prayer the Holy Prophet[sa] would continue sitting long enough to recite the following prayer:

اَللّٰهُمَّ أَنْتَ السَّلَامُ وَمِنْكَ السَّلَامُ ، تَبَارَكْتَ يَا ذَا الْجَلَالِ وَالْإِكْرَامِ

Transliteration:

Allāhumma antas-salāmu wa minkas-salāmu, tabārakta yā dhul-jalāli wal-ikrām.

Translation:

O our Lord! Thou art (the embodiment of) peace. And true peace comes from Thee. Blessed art Thou, O Lord of Majesty and Bounty. (Saḥīḥ Muslim, Kitābul-Masājid wa mawādhi'uṣ-Ṣalāta, Bāb Istiḥbābu-dhikri ba'daṣ-Ṣalāt)

It is also related in the Books of Traditions that on some occasions, the Holy Prophet[sa] used to sit among his followers and raise his hands to pray for those who requested him to pray for them. However, as is evident from what Ḥaḍrat 'Ā'ishah[ra] has related, it was not the normal practice of the Holy Prophet[sa] to raise hands in silent prayer after he had finished his *Ṣalāt*. This occasional gesture of the Holy Prophet[sa] which has been reported in some Traditions has mistakenly been generalised. The result has been that certain sects in Islam regard it as his normal practice (*Sunnah*) while in fact, according to the Sayings of the Holy Prophet[sa] mentioned above, this was not his common practice. The Ahmadiyya Muslim Community is of the view that to raise hands to pray after finishing the *Ṣalāt* was not the common practice, *Sunnah*, of the Holy Prophet[sa]. His practice was to sit for a while remembering Allah and reciting prayers without raising his hands.

Apart from the above-mentioned prayer, the

following were also recited by the Holy Prophet[sa] after Prayer:

لَآ اِلٰهَ اِلَّا اللّٰهُ وَحْدَهٗ لَا شَرِيْكَ لَهٗ۔ لَهُ الْمُلْكُ وَلَهُ الْحَمْدُ وَ

هُوَ عَلٰى كُلِّ شَيْءٍ قَدِيْرٌ

Transliteration:

Lā ilāha illallāhu waḥdahū lā sharīka lah. Lahul-mulku wa lahul ḥamd. Wa huwa 'alā kulli shai'in qadīr.

Translation:

There is no one worthy of worship except Allah. He is alone and has no partner. Sovereignty and praise are only for Him and He has full authority over everything.

اَللّٰهُمَّ لَا مَانِعَ لِمَا أَعْطَيْتَ وَلَا مُعْطِيَ لِمَا مَنَعْتَ وَلَا يَنْفَعُ ذَا

الْجَدِّ مِنْكَ الْجَدُّ

Transliteration:

Allāhumma lā māni'a lima a'ṭaita walā mu'ṭiya lima mana'ta walā yanfa'u dhal jaddi minkal jaddu. (*Ṣaḥīḥ Bukhārī, Kitābuṣ-Ṣalāt, bābu dhikri ba'daṣ-Ṣalāt*).

Translation:

O Allah! Nobody can hold back whatever You have granted and none can grant what Thou hold back. And no great person can benefit from his greatness

in opposition to Thy Greatness.

اَللّٰهُمَّ أَعِنِّي عَلٰى ذِكْرِكَ وَشُكْرِكَ وَحُسْنِ عِبَادَتِكَ

Transliteration:

Allāhumma a'innī 'alā dhikrika wa shukrika wa ḥusni 'ibādatika.

Translation:

O my Lord, help me so that I can properly perform Thy remembrance and Thy thanksgiving, and that I may worship Thee in the best possible manner.

سُبْحَانَ رَبِّكَ رَبِّ الْعِزَّةِ عَمَّا يَصِفُوْنَ، وَسَلَامٌ عَلَى الْمُرْسَلِيْنَ، وَالْحَمْدُ لِلّٰهِ رَبِّ الْعَالَمِيْنَ

Transliteration:

Subḥāna Rabbika Rabbil 'izzati 'ammā yaṣifūn, Wa salāmun 'alal-Mursalīn, Wal ḥamdu lillāhi Rabbil 'ālamīn. (Tirmidhī, Kitābuṣ-Ṣalāt, Bāb ma Yaqūlu idhā Sallama)

Translation:

Thy Lord is Holy and clear of all that is alleged against Him (by the non-believers); and He is Exalted. May God's blessing be upon all Messengers. All praise truly belongs to Allah Who is the Sustainer of all the worlds.

At the request of some Companions, the Holy

Prophet[sa] also prescribed the prayers below to glorify Allah. In some sections of the Muslim society, this has become a regular practice. It should be remembered that they do not form part of his regular precept. Therefore, it is not essential for a person to recite them after his obligatory Prayers in a mosque.

a. *Subḥānallāh*, i.e. Holy is Allah, free from all defects—to be recited thirty-three times.
b. *Alḥamdu Lillāh,* i.e. All praise belongs to Allah—to be recited thirty-three times.
c. *Allāhu Akbar,* i.e. Allah is the Greatest—to be recited thirty-four times.

4. TYPES OF PRAYERS AND NUMBER OF *RAK'ĀT*

There are four types of Prayers:

1. Farḍ *2. Wājib* *3. Sunnat* *4. Nafl*

FARḌ PRAYERS

Farḍ is an Arabic word which means compulsory or obligatory. There are five obligatory Prayers everyday:

Prayer	No. of *Rak'āt*
Fajr	2
Ẓuhr	4
'Aṣr	4
Maghrib	3
'Ishā'	4

It is sinful to leave out a *Farḍ* Prayer intentionally, but if such a Prayer is missed through forgetfulness or due to unavoidable circumstances, then this mistake can be rectified by offering the missed Prayer as soon as one remembers, or whenever possible.

WĀJIB PRAYERS

The following Prayers are regarded as *Wājib* (necessary) Prayers:

1. Three *Rak'āt* of *Vitr*.
2. Two *Rak'āt* of *'Īdul-Fiṭr* and two *Rak'āt* of *'Īdul-Aḍḥā*.
3. Two *Rak'āt* offered while performing the *Ṭawāf* of the *Ka'bah*.

If a person misses these Prayers intentionally, he is deemed to have committed a sin. However, if he misses a *Wājib* Prayer unintentionally, e.g., through forgetfulness, he is not required to offer it as a *Qaḍā* Prayer. *Qaḍā* means offering of a missed Prayer.

ṢALĀTUL-VITR

Vitr literally means odd. There are three *Rak'āt* in this Prayer. It is offered after the *'Ishā'* Prayer. It is preferable to recite *Sūrah Al-A'lā*, *Sūrah Al-Kāfirūn* and *Sūrah Al-Ikhlāṣ* respectively in these *Rak'āt*. However, this is not necessary. Any *Sūrah* or verses of the Holy Quran can be recited. In the third *Rak'at* of *Vitr*, after performing the *Rukū'*, *Du'ā'i Qunūt* should be recited which is as follows:

اَللّٰهُمَّ اِنَّا نَسْتَعِيْنُكَ وَ نَسْتَغْفِرُكَ وَ نُؤْمِنُ بِكَ وَ نَتَوَكَّلُ

عَلَيْكَ وَ نُثْنِي عَلَيْكَ الْخَيْرَ، وَنَشْكُرُكَ وَ لَا نَكْفُرُكَ وَ نَخْلَعُ

وَ نَتْرُكُ مَنْ يَفْجُرُكَ. اَللّٰهُمَّ اِيَّاكَ نَعْبُدُ وَ لَكَ نُصَلِّي وَ

نَسْجُدُ، وَ اِلَيْكَ نَسْعٰى وَ نَحْفِدُ وَ نَرْجُوْ رَحْمَتَكَ وَ نَخْشٰى

عَذَابَكَ اِنَّ عَذَابَكَ بِالْكُفَّارِ مُلْحِق۔

Transliteration:

Allāhumma innā nasta'īnuka wa nastaghfiruka, wa nu'minu bika wa natawakkalu 'alaika, wa nuthnī 'alaikal khair, wa nash-kuruka walā nakfuruka, wa nakhla'u wa natruku man-yafjuruk. Allāhumma iyyāka na'budu wa laka nuṣallī wa nasjudu, wa ilaika nas'ā wa naḥfidu, wa narjū raḥmataka, wa nakhshā 'adhābaka, Inna 'adhābaka bil kuffāri mulḥiq.

Translation:

O Allah, we beseech Thy help and ask Thy protection and believe in Thee and trust in Thee and we praise Thee in the best manner and we thank Thee and we are not ungrateful to Thee, and we cast off and forsake him who disobeys Thee. O Allah! Thee alone do we serve and to Thee alone do we pray and make obeisance and to Thee we flee and we are quick and we hope for Thy mercy and we fear Thy chastisement, for surely Thy chastisement overtakes the unbeliehers.

SUNNAT PRAYERS

The Holy Prophet[sa] of Islam offered extra *Rak'āt* of Prayer in addition to those of *Farḍ* Prayers. These Prayers are called *Sunnat* Prayers. Offering *Sunnat* Prayers is considered to be necessary by all jurists. The wilful neglect of *Sunnat* Prayers is censurable in the sight of Allah. *Sunnat* Prayers are:

1. Two *Rak'āt* before the *Farḍ* Prayer of *Fajr*; but if a person joins the congregation without having offered two *Rak'āt* of *Sunnat* due to some unavoidable circumstances, he can offer them after the congregational lead Prayer.
2. Four *Rak'āt* before *Farḍ* and two *Rak'āt* after *Farḍ* in *Ẓuhr* Prayer. In case one has not performed the four *Rak'āt* of *Sunnat* before the congregational four *Rak'āt* due to unavoidable circumstances, one should do so after the congregational Prayer.
   Note: Ahmadi Muslims, who most often follow the *Ḥanafī* school of thought, offer four *Rak'āt* of *Sunnat* before the *Farḍ* of *Ẓuhr* and two *Rak'āt* of *Sunnat* after the *Farḍ* of *Ẓuhr* Prayer. However, some other Muslims offer four *Rak'āt* of *Sunnat* before the *Farḍ* of *Ẓuhr* Prayer and four after the *Farḍ* of *Ẓuhr* Prayer.
3. Two *Rak'āt* of *Sunnat* after the *Farḍ* of *Maghrib* Prayer.
4. Two *Rak'āt* of *Sunnat* after the *Farḍ Rak'āt* of *'Ishā'* Prayer.

NAWĀFIL PRAYERS

Muslims also offer additional *Rak'āt* of Prayer

apart from *Farḍ* and *Sunnat Rak'āt*. These are called *Nawāfil* Prayers or *Nafl*.

These are optional Prayers. Those who voluntarily offer *Nawāfil* Prayers reap the benefits of Allah's favours. *Nawāfil* Prayers are as follows:

1. Eight *Rak'āt* of *Tahajjud*.
2. Two *Rak'āt* after the two *Rak'āt* of *Sunnat* at the end of *Ẓuhr* Prayer.
3. Four *Rak'āt* before *Farḍ* of *'Aṣr* Prayer.
4. Two *Rak'āt* after the two *Rak'āt* of *Sunnat* in *Maghrib* Prayer.
5. Four *Rak'āt* of *Ishrāq* Prayer.
6. Two *Rak'āt* offered when one enters a mosque.
7. Two *Rak'āt* offered when seeking blessings from God Almighty.
8. Two *Rak'āt* offered as *Ṣalāt-i-Hājjāt*.
9. Two *Rak'āt* offered as a Thanksgiving Prayer.

There are some other *Nawāfil* Prayers which are mentioned later in this book.

One may offer as many *Nawāfil* Prayers as one wishes. However, *Nawāfil* should not be offered during the forbidden times for Prayers. For example, they should not be offered between *'Aṣr* Prayer and *Maghrib* Prayer. It is preferable to offer *Nawāfil* Prayers at home rather than in a mosque except for those which have been mentioned to be offered in a mosque. However, it is a matter of personal choice and there is no compulsion in this matter.

5. *ṢALĀTUL-JUMU'AH* or FRIDAY PRAYER

Ṣalātul-Jumu'ah or Friday Prayer is offered in congregation. It is offered in place of *Ẓuhr* Prayer. Each week on Friday, Muslims are required to take a bath, dress in their best clean clothes, wear perfume and assemble in the mosque for Friday Prayer. The Holy Quran and the Hadith speak highly of the blessings of *Jumu'ah* Prayer. If a Muslim spends Friday in the remembrance of God Almighty, supplicating before his Lord, he is abundantly rewarded by Allah.

Friday Prayer is an occasion for the assembly of the Muslims of a whole city or a town. In a large city, Friday Prayer can be offered in more than one place for the convenience of the Muslim community. It gives them an opportunity to meet together to discuss and solve their individual as well as community problems. Getting together once a week develops unity, cooperation and cohesiveness among Muslims. Friday Prayer is also a demonstration of Islamic equality.

It gives the *Imām* a chance to advise all Muslims at the same time on urgent matters that face them. The *Imām's* sermon gives them guidance in Islamic teachings. Friday Prayer is an obligatory Prayer for every adult male Muslim. However, those who are sick, blind or disabled, those on a journey, and women, are exempt from the obligation of attending the Prayer at the mosque. They can join in the Prayer if they so wish, but if they cannot attend the Friday Prayer, they have to offer *Ẓuhr* Prayer instead, as the Friday Prayer is offered in place of *Ẓuhr* Prayer.

There are two *Adhāns* for Friday Prayer. The first *Adhān* is recited when the sun begins to decline and the second is recited just before the *Imām* stands up before the congregation to deliver his sermon.

The sermon consists of two parts. In the first part the *Imām*, after the recitation of *Ta'awwudh* and *Sūrah Al-Fātiḥah*, advises the gathering to act upon the commandments of Allah and also about the duties they have to perform to become good Muslims. The sermon can also deal with any other matter of importance. This part of the sermon can be delivered in any language.

After delivering the first part of the sermon, the *Imām* sits down for a short while, then stands up again and starts with the second part which is in Arabic and which reads as follows:

اَلْحَمْدُ لِلّٰهِ نَحْمَدُهٗ وَنَسْتَعِيْنُهٗ وَنَسْتَغْفِرُهٗ ،وَنُؤْمِنُ بِهٖ ، وَنَتَوَكَّلُ
عَلَيْهِ، وَنَعُوْذُ بِاللّٰهِ مِنْ شُرُوْرِ أَنْفُسِنَا وَمِنْ سَيِّئَاتِ أَعْمَالِنَا ،
مَنْ يَهْدِهِ اللّٰهُ فَلَا مُضِلَّ لَهٗ ، وَمَنْ يُّضْلِلْهُ فَلَا هَادِيَ لَهٗ ، وَنَشْهَدُ
أَنْ لَّا إِلٰهَ إِلَّا اللّٰهُ وَحْدَهٗ لَا شَرِيْكَ لَهٗ ، وَنَشْهَدُ أَنَّ مُحَمَّدًا
عَبْدُهٗ وَرَسُوْلُهٗ۔ عِبَادَ اللّٰهِ رَحِمَكُمُ اللّٰه اِنَّ اللّٰهَ يَأْمُرُ
بِالْعَدْلِ وَ الْاِحْسَانِ وَ اِيْتَآئِ ذِى الْقُرْبٰى وَ يَنْهٰى عَنِ

الْفَحْشَآءِ وَ الْمُنْكَرِ وَ الْبَغْيِ يَعِظُكُمْ لَعَلَّكُمْ
تَذَكَّرُونَ۔اُذْكُرُوا اللّٰهَ يَذْكُرْكُمْ وَادْعُوهُ يَسْتَجِبْ لَكُمْ
وَلَذِكْرُ اللّٰهِ اَكْبَرُ۔

Transliteration:

Alḥamdu lillāhi naḥmaduhū wa nasta'īnuhū wa nastaghfiruhū wa nu'minu bihī wa natawakkalu 'alaih. Wa na'ūdhu Billāhi min shurūri anfusinā wamin sayyi'āti a'mālinā. Man-yahdihillāhu falā muḍilla lahū wa man-yuḍlilhu falā hādiya lah. Wa nash-hadu allā ilāha illallāhu waḥdahū lā sharīka lahū wa nash-hadu anna Muḥmmadan 'abduhū wa Rasūluh. 'Ibādallāhi raḥima-kumullāh. Innallāha ya'muru bil 'adli wal-iḥsāni wa ītāi' dhil-qurbā, wa yanhā 'anil faḥshāi' wal-munkari wal-baghyi, Ya'iẓukum la'allakum tadhakkarūn. Udhkurullāh yadh-kur-kum wad'ūhu yastajib lakum. Wala Dhikrullāhi Akbar.

Translation:

All praise is due to Allah. We laud Him, we beseech help from Him and ask His protection; we confide in Him, we trust Him alone and we seek protection against the evils and mischief of our souls and from the bad results of our deeds. Whomsoever He guides on the right path, none can misguide him; and whosoever He declares misled, none can guide him onto the right path. And we bear witness that none deserves to be worshipped except Allah. He is alone and has no partner. We bear witness that Muhammad is His servant and Messenger. O servants of Allah! May Allah be Merciful to you. Verily, Allah commands you to act with justice, to confer benefits upon each other and to do good to others as one does to one's kindred and forbids evil which pertain to your own selves and evils which affect others and prohibits revolts against a lawful authority. He warns you against being unmindful. You remember Allah; He too will remember you; call Him and He will make a response to your call. And verily divine remembrance is the highest virtue.

Muslims are required to listen to the sermon attentively. Any type of conversation during the sermon is prohibited. After the *Imām* has delivered the second part of the sermon, the *Iqāmah* is recited and the *Imām* leads the congregational two *Rak'āt* of *Jumu'ah* Prayer.

The Holy Prophet[sa] of Islam did not approve of a person telling others to refrain from conversation while the *Imām* is delivering his Sermon. In unavoidable circumstances, a gesture by hand or with a finger can be made to draw the attention of someone to stop talking. In case the *Imām* asks something during the sermon, then he should be replied to.

It is preferable that the person who delivered the sermon should lead the Prayer. The *Imām* should recite *Sūrah Al-Fātiḥah* and some verses of the Holy Quran in a loud voice during the *Jumu'ah* Prayer. One should offer four *Rak'āt* of *Sunnat* Prayer before the Friday congregational Prayer and four *Rak'āt* of *Sunnat* after the congregational *Jumu'ah* Prayer, but two *Rak'āt* of *Sunnat* after the congregational and *Farḍ Jumu'ah* Prayer are also allowed instead of four, as mentioned in the famous book of Traditions called *Sunan Abū Dawūd* (*Kitābuṣ-Ṣalāt, Bāb Aṣ-Ṣalāt ba'dal Jumu'ah wash-sharah As-Sunnah*, Vol.3 page 449). The two *Rak'āt* of *Sunnat* Prayer to be offered before the *Farḍ* are compulsory and are not dropped even during a journey.

A person who comes to the mosque during the sermon should not steer his way to the front by jumping over the shoulders of the people already sitting. As the sermon has already begun, he can if he wishes, offer two *Rak'āt* of *Sunnat* quickly during the sermon. If a person is late for Friday Prayer and joins the congregation in the final *Qa'dah*, he should complete his Prayer individually after the *Imām* has finished leading the Prayer. If, however, he misses the congregational Prayer completely, such a person should offer *Ẓuhr* Prayer instead.

6. *'ĪDUL-FIṬR* AND *'ĪDUL-AḌḤĀ* FESTIVALS

There are two *'Īd* festivals in a year. One is called *'Īdul-Fiṭr* and the other, which comes about 10 weeks later is called *'Īdul-Aḍḥā*. *'Īdul-Fiṭr* is celebrated at the end of the month of fasting. On this day, Muslims rejoice for having been given the strength to fulfil their obligation of fasting.

'Īdul-Aḍḥā is celebrated on the 10th of the month of *Dhul-Ḥajj* to commemorate the obedience of Ḥaḍrat Ibrāhīm[as] (Abraham) and his son Ḥaḍrat Ishmael[as] (Ismā'īl). Allah accepted the devotion and obedience of both of them and directed that a lamb be sacrificed instead of Ḥaḍrat Ishmael[as]. Muslims who gather in Makkah for *Ḥajj*, offer their sacrifices on the occasion of *'Īdul-Aḍḥā*, following the example of Prophet Ibrāhīm[as]. This act of sacrificing animals is repeated by Muslims all over the world.

All Muslims, men, women, and children, join in the congregational two *Rak'āt* Prayer held in the open outside a village or town, if possible, on both *'Īdul-Fiṭr* and *'Īdul-Aḍḥā* occasions.

Early in the morning, on an *'Īd* day, after taking a bath, Muslims, young and old, put on their best clothes. Children specially, wear new garments. Perfume is worn by men and women alike, as it was the practice of the Holy Prophet[sa] to wear perfume on such occasion. Specially dishes are prepared on *'Īd* days in Muslim homes.

On the occasion of *'Īdul-Fiṭr*, one should pay *Fiṭrānah* before the *'Īd* Prayer. *Fiṭrānah* is spent on the poor and needy so that they, too, can join in the festivities of *'Īd*. Every member of the household is required to contribute towards the *Fiṭrānah* at the rate fixed for that year. *Fiṭrānah* is due in respect of children also, even of newborn babies, whose parents are expected to make the nescessary payments. One should have a full breakfast before proceeding to the *'Īd-gāh*, the place where *'Īd* Prayer is offered. On the occasion of *'Īdul-Aḍḥā*, it is reported that the Holy Prophet[sa] preferred not to eat anything until he slaughtered his own animal for sacrifice. With the meat of that sacrifice he would have the first meal of the day, but to eat before that is not forbidden.

As was the practice of the Holy Prophet[sa] Muslims generally go to the *'Īd-gāh* by one route and return by another route.

The time for *'Īd* Prayer is before noon. Like Friday Prayer, *'Īd* Prayer is always offered in congregation. No *Adhān* or *Iqāmah* is called for *'Īd* Prayers.

In the first *Rak'at* of *'Īd* Prayer, after reciting *Takbīr-i-Taḥrīmah* and *Thanā'*, but before reciting *Ta'awwudh* the *Imām* raises his hands to his earlobes seven times saying *Allāhu Akbar* each time in a loud voice and then drops his arms to his side each time until after the seventh *Takbīr* when he folds his arms the normal fashion and proceeds with the Prayer. The followers also raise their hands to their earlobes saying *Allāhu Akbar* but in an inaudible voice and then leave their hands hanging by their sides as done by the *Imām*. In the second *Rak'at* there are five *Takbīrāt*, i.e. the *Imām* and the followers raise their hands to their ears five times saying *Allāhu Akbar* and then leaving them hanging on their sides each time.

At the end of second *Rak'at*, after the recitation of *Tashahhud*, and *Durūd* and some of the prescribed Prayers, the *Imām* turns his face towards the right saying *Assalāmu 'Alaikum wa Raḥmatullāh* and then turns his face to the left saying the same, to mark the end of the Prayer.

After the *'Īd* Prayer, the *Imām* delivers a sermon. Like for the Friday Prayer, *'Īd* sermon consists of two parts. It should be noted that the sermon for the Friday Prayer precedes the Prayer, while on the occasion of *'Īd*, the sermon follows the Prayer.

After the two *Rak'āt* of *'Īdul-Aḍḥā* Prayer, the *Imām* and the congregation recite the following words of glorification of God in an audible voice:

اَللّٰهُ اَكْبَرُ اللّٰهُ اَكْبَرُ، لَا اِلٰهَ اِلَّا اللّٰهُ وَاللّٰهُ اَكْبَرُ اللّٰهُ اَكْبَرُ وَ لِلّٰهِ

الْحَمْدُ۔

Transliteration:

Allāhu Akbar, Allāhu Akbar, lā ilāha illallāhu wallāhu akbar Allāhu Akbar, wa lillāhil ḥamd.

Translation:

Allah is the Greatest; Allah is the Greatest. There is none worthy of worship except Allah; Allah is the Greatest, Allah is the Greatest and all Praise belongs to Him.

Similarly, from the time of *Fajr* Prayer on the 9th *Dhul-Ḥajj* till the *'Aṣr* time of the 13th of *Dhul-Ḥajj*, loud recitations of the above verses are made after each congregational *Farḍ* Prayer service.

Note: To recite the above-mentioned verses while

going to the *'Īd-gāh* and while coming back, is to follow the practice of the Holy Prophet[sa] of Islam.

7. CONSTITUENT PARTS OF PRAYER

The functions performed in a Prayer are categorised according to their relative importance.

FARḌ (COMPULSORY) PARTS OF PRAYER

Those which are so essential that without them the Prayer cannot be considered valid, are called *Farḍ*, i.e. obligatory, mandatory or compulsory.

If *Farḍ* constituent parts are not carried out, the Prayer becomes null and void. However, in case a worshipper does not perform that part because he completely forgot about it, the Prayer will be held valid in the sight of Allah. If he had forgotten at the time but remembers it either during the Prayer or after the Prayer, or if someone reminds him of his omission, then he should rectify the omission by performing the function that has been missed and then perform the *Sujūd-us-Sahv*, i.e. two prostrations by way of condonement. These compulsory functions are as follows:

1. *Takbīr-i-Taḥrīmah*: To say *Allāhu Akbar* to begin the Prayer.
2. *Qiyām*: The posture of Standing.
3. *Rukū'*: The posture of Bowing down.
4. *Sajdah*: The posture of Prostrating. The above are the common features of every *Rak'at*.
5. The Final *Qa'dah*: The last long sitting position before ending the Prayer. This feature is not

repeated in every *Rak'at*.

6. Recitation of *Sūrah Al-Fātiḥah*: The recitation of *Sūrah Al-Fātiḥah* is also essential in every *Rak'at*.

When the *Imām* is leading the congregation, the loud recitation of *Sūrah Al-Fātiḥah* is compulsory in the first two *Rak'āt* of the following Prayers:

a. *Fajr* Prayer, which comprises two *Rak'āt*.
b. *Maghrib* Prayer, which comprises three *Rak'āt*.
c. *'Ishā'* Prayer, which comprises four *Rak'āt*.

Note: If the recitation of some portion of the Holy Quran is not done in the first two *Rak'āt*, the *Rak'āt* will not be invalidated, but on remembering this mistake, the two *Sujūd-us-Sahv* become essential to validate the Prayer. If the *Imām* forgets to recite *Sūrah Al-Fātiḥah* aloud and also the additional verses of the Holy Quran in any *Rak'at*, and he is reminded of this before he goes to the Bowing position, he should complete this function by reciting *Sūrah Al-Fātiḥah* as well as the verses of the Holy Quran and then go into *Rukū'*. In this case no prostrations of condonement are necessary. However, if he has led the congregation into *Rukū'* and then remembers his mistake, the repetition of the function, i.e. the recitation of *Sūrah Al-Fātiḥah* and the verses of the Holy Quran, is not needed. Only two Prostrations of condonement are enough to make the Prayer valid.

WĀJIBĀT (ESSENTIALS) OF THE *ṢALĀT*

The *Wājibāt* (essential or necessary parts) is the second category. These are the parts which, if left out wilfully, will invalidate the Prayer, but if forgotten and remembered afterwards, may be condoned by offering two Prostrations of condonement towards the end of the Prayer. The Prostrations of condonement are deemed sufficient to rectify the mistake and the missed function is not repeated in this case. The *Wājibāt* of the Prayer are as follows:

1. The recitation of a portion of the Holy Quran after reciting *Sūrah Al-Fātiḥah* in the first two *Rak'āt* of the *Farḍ* part of the Prayer and in all *Sunnat* and *Nawāfil* Prayers.
2. Standing erect after *Rukū'*, technically called *Qaumah*. Note: *Qiyām* is a *Farḍ* part, i.e. is compulsory, while *Qaumah* is *Wājib* i.e. essential or necessary.
3. *Jilsah*, the sitting position between two prostrations.
4. Short sitting position after completing the first two *Rak'āt* (not the final *Qa'dah*).
5. Recite *Tashahhud,* i.e. *At-taḥiyyātu Lillāhi waṣ-Ṣalawātu*.....in *Qa'dah* position.
6. For the *Imām* to recite *Sūrah Al-Fātiḥah* and a portion of the Holy Quran audibly in the first two *Rak'āt* of *Fajr*, *Maghrib*, *'Ishā'*, *Jumu'ah* and *'Īd* Prayers, and to recite the same silently in *Ẓuhr* and *'Aṣr* Prayers.
7. *Tartīb*, i.e. to perform various *Farḍ* and *Wājib* parts of the *Ṣalāt* in their appropriate order.
8. *Ta'dīl* i.e. to perform all parts of the Prayer with dignity and respect. In other words the *Ṣalāt* (Prayer) should be offered with full concentration and without any haste.

9. To turn the face to the right and to the left, saying *Assalāmu 'Alaikum wa Raḥmatullāh*, to mark the end of the Prayer.
10. For the *Imām* to say *Takbīr-i-Taḥrīmah* aloud.

SUNAN (PLURAL OF *SUNNAT*) OF THE *ṢALĀT*

All other parts of the *Ṣalāt*, besides the *Farḍ* and *Wājib* constituents, are either *Sunnat* or *Mustaḥab* factors. The worshipper should strictly adhere to all the *Sunnat* and *Mustaḥab* parts of the *Ṣalāt* and should not omit any of them without any good reason. However, no prostrations of condonement are performed if any of the *Sunnat* or *Mustaḥab* parts are omitted. The *Sunnat* parts of the *Ṣalāt* (Prayer) are as follows:

1. To raise the hands up to the ear lobes when reciting *Takbīr-i-Taḥrīmah*.
2. Folding of arms in *Qiyām* position.
3. To recite *Thanā'*.
4. To recite *Ta'awwudh* before reciting *Sūrah Al-Fātiḥah*.
5. To say *Āmīn* at the end of *Sūrah Al-Fātiḥah*.
6. To say *Allāhu Akbar* while going to *Rukū'*.
7. To recite *Subḥāna Rabbiyal 'Aẓīm* at least three times in *Rukū'* position.
8. To say *Sami'allāhu liman Ḥamidah* while getting up from *Rukū'*, and in case one is offering individual Prayer, to say *Rabbanā wa lakal Ḥamd*. If one is following the *Imām* in a congregation, to say *Rabbanā wa lakal Ḥamd* is the Practice of the Holy Prophet[sa].

9. To say *Allāhu Akbar* while going into the position of Prostration and while getting up from the Prostration.
10. To say *Subḥāna Rabbiyal A'lā* at least three times during the Prostration.
11. To recite the prescribed prayer during the *Jilsah* position.
12. To raise the forefinger of the right hand while reciting *Ashhadu allā illāha Illallāh*.
13. To recite *Durūd* and other prayers during the final *Qa'dah*.
14. To recite *Sūrah Al-Fātiḥah* in the third and fourth *Rak'at*.
15. For the *Imām* to say *Allāhu Akbar*, and *Sami'allāhu liman Ḥamidah*, in an audible voice.

MUSTAḤIBBĀT OF THE *ṢALĀT*

The following things, which pertain to the style and the carriage of Prayer, i.e. its beauty and its excellence, are entitled *Mustaḥibbāt* of the Prayer. The term *Mustaḥibbāt* means preferable and praiseworthy. Of course, they are not compulsory, essential or *Sunnat* parts of the Prayer. They are as follows:

1. To fix one's gaze on the spot which will be touched by the head during prostration.
2. To place one's hands on the knees with spread fingers while performing *Rukū'*.
3. To leave one's hands by one's sides in *Qaumah* position.
4. To prostrate in such a manner that the knees

touch the ground first, then the hands, the nose and the forehead.

5. To get up from the second *Rak'at* after Prostration without any support.
6. To place one's hands on one's lap near the knees so that the fingers are spread towards the *Qiblah.*
7. To sit on the left foot in *Qa'dah* and *Jilsah* position, and to plant the right foot in a way that the toes are towards the *Qiblah.*
8. After the recitation of *Sūrah Al-Fātiḥah*, the Quranic verses which are recited should be longer in the first *Rak'at* as compared to the verses recited in the second *Rak'at.*
9. For the worshipper who is following the *Imām*, to say *Āmīn* in an audible voice and to say *Rabbanā wa lakal Ḥamd* in an inaudible voice.

MAKRŪHĀT OF THE *ṢALĀT* (UNDESIRABLE ACTS DURING PRAYER)

These are acts which are undesirable, and are below the dignity of the Prayer. Prayer should always be offered with a consciousness that one is standing before one's Lord. The *Makrūhāt* are:

1. To fiddle with one's clothing.
2. To glance sideways or to the sky.
3. To keep the eyes closed.
4. To offer Prayer without any head dress.
5. Not to place one's feet with toes towards the *Qiblah* during Prostration or to lift the feet from the ground in this position.
6. To start Prayer when one is hungry whilst food is

laid on the table.

7. To continue the Prayer in spite of an urge to go to the toilet.
8. To pray in a cemetery while facing a grave.
9. To offer Prayer in very tight clothes so that one feels uncomfortable during the Prayer.
10. To pray in an unsuitable environment, e.g., in a stable, goat's pen or in a noisy market place.
11. To stand with one's weight shifted on to one leg alone or to do things which are below the dignity of the Prayer.
12. To pray in an open place without a *Sutra*. A *Sutra* is an object placed before the worshipper to mark the boundary of his Prayer.
13. To nod when someone says *Assalāmu 'Alaikum* during the Prayer.
14. To pray without washing one's mouth after eating.
15. To change the order of *Sūrahs* in the Prayer, i.e. to recite *Sūrahs* which come later in the Quran in the first *Rak'at* and the *Sūrahs* which appear earlier in the Holy Quran, in the following *Rak'āt*.
16. To place hands under the forehead while in prostration.
17. To rest one's belly on things during prostration.
18. To spread one's forearms on the ground while performing *Sajdah*.
19. To recite Quranic verses during *Rukū'* or *Sajdah*.
20. To go ahead of the *Imām*, i.e. to go into the next posture before the *Imām*.

Note 1: A worshipper is allowed to remove or kill any harmful insect in case he finds it close to where he is praying.

Note 2: The place of worship should be neat and clean and the air, as far as possible, should be free of any unpleasant odour. Every Muslim is enjoined to respect the dignity of the Prayer even if he is not praying himself. No one should in any way, e.g. by words of mouth or by his action, cause any worshipper discomfort or distraction. That is why it is not allowed to cross the path of a worshipper. This means that one should wait until the worshipper finishes his Prayer.

ACTIONS WHICH MAKE PRAYER NULL AND VOID

The following acts are incompatible with Prayer and invalidate Prayer if done:

1. When the ablution lapses.
2. Eating or drinking while offering Prayer.
3. To speak or to respond to anyone during Prayer.
4. To laugh during Prayer.
5. To turn the face to the right or to the left while praying.

SUJŪDUS-SAHV, i.e. PROSTRATIONS OF CONDONEMENT

If a person commits a mistake during Prayer, which affects the validity of the Prayer, e.g. if he is in doubt whether he has offered the prescribed number of *Rak'āt*, the Prostrations of condonement are necessary.

The Prostrations are offered after the recitation of *Tashahhud*, and *Durūd*, and other prescribed prayers in the final *Qa'dah* of the Prayer. Thus, after saying *Allāhu Akbar*, two prostrations are performed, in which *Subḥāna Rabbiyal A'lā* is recited, then the *Imām* reverts back to *Qa'dah* position and says *Assalāmu 'Alaikum wa Raḥmatullāh* turning his face towards the right and then towards the left, to mark the end of the Prayer.

If the *Imām* commits such a mistake which can be condoned by the Prostrations, then the whole congregation will have to perform those Prostrations of condonement. But if one of the followers commits a mistake while following the *Imām*, he is not required to perform the Prostrations of condonement.

If there is a doubt as to how many *Rak'āt* have been performed, then one should observe the rule of certainty, i.e. if the doubt is whether one has offered three or four *Rak'āt*, for instance, one should offer the fourth *Rak'at* to be on the safe side though one might have offered it before.

8. PRAYER OFFERED IN EXCEPTIONAL CIRCUMSTANCES

PRAYER DURING SICKNESS

The performance of *Ṣalāt* is of prime importance in Islam. A sick person who cannot stand for Prayer, should offer his Prayer while sitting; and if he cannot even sit, he should offer his Prayer while lying down.

If he cannot bow down or prostrate, he is allowed to make symbolic gestures to that effect, and if he is so sick that he cannot move his head or hand, he can fulfill this obligation by making gestures in his mind.

PRAYER DURING A JOURNEY

If a person is travelling by any means of transportation which precludes his standing up for Prayer, nor can he get off from the vehicle, he can offer his Prayer while seated and the condition of facing towards the *Qiblah* would not be mandatory in this situation. He should face in the direction in which the mount, vehicle, boat or airplane, etc., is moving, if possible.

In the early days of Islam, the *Ẓuhr, 'Aṣr* and *'Ishā'* congregational Prayer services had only two *Rak'āt*, just like *Fajr* Prayer but subsequently they continued to be of two *Rak'āt* length only for a person who is on a journey. In normal circumstances, the number of *Rak'āt* were doubled. Hence, normally, one has to perform four *Rak'āt Farḍ* each, for *Ẓuhr*, *'Aṣr* and *'Ishā'* Prayers while a traveller offers only two *Rak'āt* for each of the above-mentioned Prayers.

If a traveller reaches a place where he intends to stay less than 15 days, then this concession will apply and he will shorten his Prayers as mentioned above.

However, this concession does not apply to the *Farḍ* part of the *Fajr* and *Maghrib* Prayers.

If a person is staying with a close relative whose house he regards as his own, e.g. his parents' home, the home of his in-laws, or a religious headquarter such as Makkah, Medina, Qadian or Rabwah, etc., he can shorten his Prayer as outlined above but it would be preferable for him to offer the full four *Rak'āt* as applicable.

While one is on a journey, the *Sunnat* part of every Prayer is dropped, with the exception of the *Vitr Rak'āt* in the *'Ishā'* Prayer and the two *Rak'āt Sunnat* of the *Fajr* Prayer.

To offer *Nawāfil* during a journey, i.e. optional Prayers, are entirely up to each individual.

Moreover, it is also permissible to combine two Prayer services during a journey. *Ẓuhr* Prayer can be joined with the *'Aṣr* Prayer and can both be offered either at the *Ẓuhr* Prayer time or at *'Aṣr* Prayer time. Similarly the *'Ishā'* Prayer can be joined with the *Maghrib* Prayer and can be offered either at *Maghrib* Prayer time or *'Ishā'* Prayer time.

If travellers are offering their congregational Prayer behind an *Imām* who is a local inhabitant, they have to follow the *Imām* and offer four *Rak'āt* for *Ẓuhr*, *'Aṣr* and *'Ishā'* Prayers. The rule of concession would not apply in that case. But if the person leading the Prayer, i.e. the *Imām*, is a traveller, then he will shorten his Prayer accordingly and the travellers in the congregation will also finish their Prayer with the *Imām*, while those who are not on a journey will stand up when the *Imām* has recited the salutations to mark the end of Prayer and complete their Prayer.

PRAYER DURING DANGER (*ṢALĀTUL-KHAUF*)

It is permissible to shorten one's Prayer when one is facing life-threatening danger, e.g., war. The act of *Qaṣr*, which means shortening of Prayer, can be applied to Prayer in eleven different ways that have been mentioned in the Holy Quran and in the Traditions. In essence, when heavy fighting breaks out in the battlefield, or one anticipates a surprise attack from the enemy, or if the army is forced to take up positions in trenches, Prayers are shortened because of the intensity of the situation. If the situation permits one to offer two *Rak'āt*, one should offer two *Rak'āt*, otherwise one *Rak'at* would be acceptable. In case it is too dangerous to offer Prayer in congregation, individual Prayers should be offered but if the situation does not allow even this, then one can offer Prayer while on the move, on foot or on a mount, whether or not facing the *Qiblah*. If the danger is even of a greater degree, the Prayers can be offered through mere gestures, or by declaring the intention to pray and with a few gestures reciting some portion of the prescribed verses. It is also permissible to combine several Prayers at a time during such conditions. (*Ṣaḥīḥ Bukhārī, Kitābul-Maghāzī, Bāb Ghazwah Khandaq, Ṣaḥīḥ Muslim, Kitābuṣ-Ṣalāt Bāb Ṣalātul-Khauf*)

QAḌĀ (MISSED) PRAYERS

If one misses the timely performance of a daily Prayer service, e.g., due to forgetfulness, falling asleep, or becoming unconscious, etc., then such missed Prayers, when offered later on, are known as *Qaḍā* Prayers. One has to offer the obligatory part of the Prayer services which have been missed. Whenever a person realises that he has missed the obligatory Prayers or Prayer, he should offer them immediately keeping in view the natural sequence of those Prayers.

Some religious leaders have given decrees that one may offer one substitute Prayer to compensate all Prayers missed in one's lifetime. They have coined the term *Qaḍā'i 'Umrī* for it. Because of such teachings people have become less attentive in the observance of Prayers.

Prayer is the daily sustenance of the spirit. How can a person stay hungry for ten years and then eat ten years' worth of food in one go? It, therefore, demeans the institution of Prayer to suggest that a person may neglect the duty of offering Prayer all his life and then simply offer *Qaḍā'i 'Umrī* one day to compensate the loss. This is not the teaching of the Holy Prophet[sa] of Islam.

According to Islamic jurisprudence, if someone has missed a Prayer knowingly and deliberately, no *Qaḍā* can compensate that and the Prayer is lost for ever, but the true judge in such cases is God Almighty.

TAHAJJUD PRAYER

To go to bed soon after the *'Ishā'* Prayer and to get up in the late hours of the night for the observance of the optional *Tahajjud* Prayer is a source of great blessing. Although it is not obligatory, it is very strongly emphasised by the Holy Quran. It has always been the practice of the pious people to perform this Prayer regularly in order to gain Allah's special favours. The time for *Tahajjud* Prayer finishes when the time for *Fajr* Prayer starts. The supplications made during *Tahajjud* Prayer are granted acceptance by God Almighty readily. It is also a vehicle for achieving nearness to God, because at that hour, one gives up sleep and forsakes the comfort of one's bed, to fall prostrate before one's Lord. *Tahajjud* Prayer consists of eight *Rak'āt*. The Holy Prophet[sa] always offered *Tahajjud* Prayer, dividing it into two *Rak'āt* units. He used to recite long passages from the Holy Quran in the *Qiyām* position and prolong *Rukū'* and *Sajdah* with supplications. His *Tahajjud* Prayer was followed by three *Rak'āt* of *Vitr* Prayer. Thus he used to offer eleven *Rak'āt* every night before dawn.

TARĀVĪḤ PRAYER

Tarāvīḥ Prayer is the special Prayer ordained for the month of Ramadan. It has to be performed each night during the month of Ramadan. It is in fact offered at *Tahajjud* time. The observance of *Tarāvīḥ* Prayer after the *'Ishā'* Prayer was allowed during the caliphate of Ḥaḍrat 'Umar[ra], to enable such people, who for unavoidable reasons could not perform *Tarāvīḥ* Prayer at *Tahajjud* time to still offer this Prayer. However, it is preferable to offer this Prayer in pre-dawn hours. The recitation of long passages from the Holy Quran during the *Tarāvīḥ* Prayer has been in vogue among Muslims, following the practice of the

Companions of the Holy Prophet[sa].

Tarāvīḥ Prayer consists of eight *Rak'āt*, but one can offer as many as twenty or more *Rak'āt* if one wants to. It seems appropriate to take a little rest each time after offering four *Rak'āt*.

PRAYER WHEN SOLAR AND LUNAR ECLIPSES OCCUR

The solar eclipse is called *Kusūf* and the lunar eclipse is called *Khusūf.* This visual change in the heavenly bodies reminds the faithful that just as the sun and the moon appear to have lost their light to a considerable extent during the eclipses, so can various kinds of spiritual ills result in a reduction of the spiritual light that illuminates the believer's heart. Only God's mercy can protect one from such a spiritual eclipse. Hence a two *Rak'āt* Prayer is precribed on the occasion of solar or lunar eclipses as a reminder to believers that they should seek God's blessings and God's mercy if they want to scale spiritual heights.

The inhabitants of a town or city offer two *Rak'āt* in congregation, either in a mosque or outside in the open. *Sūrah Al-Fātiḥah* and long passages from the Holy Quran should be recited aloud in this Prayer. In every *Rak'at*, two *Rukū'* are performed. After the recitation of some passages of the Holy Quran, a *Rukū'* should be performed, then the *Imām* should go back in *Qiyām* position and recite some other passages from the Quran and then go into *Rukū'* for the second time. Some Traditions even tell us that the

Holy Prophet[sa] performed three *Rukū‘* in one *Rak‘at*. Then the *Imām* should go into *Sajdah* position. Lengthy supplications should be made in *Rukū‘* as well as in *Sajdah* of this Prayer. At the end of the Prayer, the *Imām* should deliver a sermon, in which he should draw the attention of people to the subject of asking forgiveness from God Almighty and he should discuss ways and means of reforming society.

PRAYER TO INVOKE RAIN

When there is a drought due to lack of rain, people might invite the mercy of God Almighty by gathering in an open field for Prayer, during the day. The *Imām* should wear a sheet of cloth as his outer garment and lead a two *Rak‘āt* Prayer. The recitation in this Prayer should also be aloud. After the Prayer, the *Imām* should lead the congregation by raising his hands in Prayer and he should recite the following:

اَللّٰهُمَّ اسْقِنَا غَيْثًا مُّغِيْثًا مُّرِيْعًا، نَّافِعًا غَيْرَ ضَآرٍّ، عَاجِلًا غَيْرَ
آجِلٍ - اَللّٰهُمَّ اسْقِ عِبَادَكَ وَبَهَآئِمَكَ وَانْشُرْ رَحْمَتَكَ
وَاَحْيِ بَلَدَكَ الْمَيِّتَ- اَللّٰهُمَّ اسْقِنَا، اَللّٰهُمَّ اسْقِنَا-

Transliteration:

Allāhummasqinā ghaitham-mughītham-murī‘an-nāfi‘an ghaira dhārin, ‘ājilan ghaira ājil. Allāhummasqi ‘ibādaka wa bahā’imaka wanshur raḥmataka wa aḥyi baladakal-mayyita. Allāhummasqinā, Allāhummasqinā. (*Sunan Abī Dāwūd,*

Kitābuṣ-Ṣalāt; Sunan Nasa'ī)

Translation:

O Allah, give us rain, abundant, widespread, producing herbage, benefiting without doing injury, soon, without delay. O Lord send water for Thy servants, and Thy animals, and extend Thy Mercy and revive the land that lies dead. O Lord send us water! O Lord send us water.

Then, the *Imām* should recite *Durūd* and continue to pray, expressing his humility and extolling the greatness of God. Then he should turn his sheet of cloth inside out. This amounts to a good omen and, in a way, depicts the plight of the people to the Creator, making a plea to Him that as the *Imām* has overturned his outer garment, God Almighty should accept their supplications and overturn the existing suffering caused by drought.

ISTIKHĀRAH PRAYER

It is a Prayer to seek guidance from God Almighty when one intends to embark upon any important task or project, e.g., trade, journey, marriage, etc. The matter may be religious or otherwise. The purpose of this Prayer is also to seek God's help so that the outcome of the task in hand is successful.

A two *Rak'āt* Prayer is offered, before one goes to bed at night, in which *Sūrah Al-Fātiḥah* is followed by *Sūrah Al-Kāfirūn* in the first *Rak'at* and *Sūrah Al-Fātiḥah* followed by *Sūrah- Al-Ikhlāṣ* in the second *Rak'at*. During *Qa'dah* position after reciting

Tashahhud and *Durūd* and some other Prayers, the following should be recited:

اَللّٰهُمَّ اِنِّیْ اَسْتَخِیْرُكَ بِعِلْمِكَ وَاَسْتَقْدِرُكَ بِقُدْرَتِكَ

وَاَسْاَلُكَ مِنْ فَضْلِكَ الْعَظِیْمِ فَاِنَّكَ تَقْدِرُوَلَا اَقْدِرُ وَتَعْلَمُ

وَلَا اَعْلَمُ وَاَنْتَ عَلَّامُ الْغُیُوْبِ۔ اَللّٰهُمَّ اِنْ كُنْتَ تَعْلَمُ

اَنَّ هٰذَا الْاَمْرَخَیْرٌ لِّیْ فِیْ دِیْنِیْ وَمَعَاشِیْ وَعَاقِبَةِ اَمْرِیْ

فَاقْدِرْهُ لِیْ وَیَسِّرْهُ لِیْ ثُمَّ بَارِكْ لِیْ فِیْهِ وَ اِنْ كُنْتَ تَعْلَمُ

اَنَّ هٰذَا الْاَمْرَ شَرٌّ لِّیْ فِیْ دِیْنِیْ وَمَعَاشِیْ وَعَاقِبَةِ اَمْرِیْ

فَاصْرِفْهُ عَنِّیْ وَاصْرِفْنِیْ عَنْهُ، وَاقْدِرْ لِیَ الْخَیْرَ حَیْثُ كَانَ

ثُمَّ اَرْضِنِیْ بِهٖ۔

Transliteration:

Allāhumma innī astakhīruka bi'ilmika wa astaqdiruka biqudratika wa as'aluka min faḍlikal 'aẓīm. Fa innaka taqdiru walā aqdiru, wa ta'lamu walā a'lamu wa anta 'allāmul ghuyūb. Allāhumma in kunta ta'lamu anna hādhal amra khairun lī fī dīnī wa ma'āshī wa 'āqibati amrī faqdirhu lī wa yassirhu lī thumma bārik lī fīh. Wa in kunta ta'lamu anna hādhal amra sharrullī fī dīnī wa ma'āshī wa 'āqibati amrī faṣrifhu 'annī waṣrifnī 'anhu, waqdir liyal-khaira ḥaithu kāna thumma arḍinī bih.

Translation:

O Allah, I seek good from Thee out of Thy knowledge and seek power from Thee out of Thy power and I beg of Thee out of Thy boundless Grace, for Thou hast power and I have no power, and Thou hast knowledge and I have no knowledge, and Thy knowledge encompasses the unseen.

O Allah! If it be within Thy knowledge that this task is for my good, both materially and spiritually, and in respect of my ultimate end, then make it possible for me and bless me therein, but if it be within Thy knowledge that it is harmful for me in my spiritual and material life and in respect of my ultimate end, then turn me away therefrom, and enable me to attain good wherever it may be and cause me to be blessed therewith. (Bukhārī, Kitābud-Da'wāt Bābud-Du'ā indal Istikhārah; Also Tirmidhī; Sharaḥ As-Sunnah Vol. 4, page 153).

This sequence of Prayer recitation is derived from the practice of the Holy Prophet[sa].

ṢALĀTUL-ḤĀJJĀT, i.e. PRAYERS OFFERED WHEN IN NEED OF HELP

This Prayer is performed when one is in need or in difficulty. The Holy Prophet[sa] said that whoever is in need of something, should perform *Wuḍū'* and then say two *Rak'āt* of Prayer. After the Prayer, one should recite *Thanā'* or glorification and praise of God Almighty, *Durūd* and then recite the prayer given below. It is hoped that the particular need will be fulfilled and God would show the way for the achievement of that goal.

لَا اِلٰهَ اِلَّا اللّٰهُ الْحَلِيْمُ الْكَرِيْمُ، سُبْحَانَ اللّٰهِ رَبِّ الْعَرْشِ
الْعَظِيْمِ۔ اَلْحَمْدُ لِلّٰهِ رَبِّ الْعَالَمِيْنَ، اَسْأَلُكَ مُوْجِبَاتِ
رَحْمَتِكَ وَعَزَائِمَ مَغْفِرَتِكَ وَالْغَنِيْمَةَ مِنْ كُلِّ بِرٍّ
وَّالسَّلَامَةَ مِنْ كُلِّ اِثْمٍ لَّا تَدَعْ لِيْ ذَنْبًا اِلَّا غَفَرْتَهٗ وَلَا هَمًّا اِلَّا
فَرَّجْتَهٗ وَلَا حَاجَةً هِيَ لَكَ رِضًا اِلَّا قَضَيْتَهَا يَا اَرْحَمَ
الرَّاحِمِيْنَ.

Transliteration:

Lā ilāha illallāhul Ḥalīmul Karīm, subḥānallāhi Rabbil 'arshil 'aẓīm. Alḥamdu lillāhi Rabbil 'ālamīn. As'aluka mūjibāti raḥmatika wa 'azā'ima maghfiratika, wal ghanīmata min kulli birrin was-salāmata min kulli ithm. Lā tada' lī dhamban illā ghafartahū wa lā hamman illā farrajtahū wa lā ḥājatan hiya laka riḍan illā qaḍaitahā yā Arḥamar-Rāḥimīn.

Translation:

There is none worthy of worship except Allah. He is the Compassionate, the Kind. Allah is free of all blemishes and holds the great Heavenly Throne. All praise belongs to Allah alone, Lord of the worlds.

Lord! I seek from Thee the instruments of Thy Mercy and the ways and means of Thy forgiveness. I implore Thee to grant me abundantly from Thy virtue and I beg Thee to keep me away from every sin. O Most Merciful God! Eliminate all my sins by forgiving them, and all my grief by dispelling it, and fulfil all my needs which Thou art pleased with.

ISHRĀQ PRAYER

This *Nawāfil* (optional) Prayer consists of two phases; offering two *Rak'āt* when the sun has risen for a while but not enough to have heated up the environment. Once the latter has occurred, this is the second phase, in which one may offer four or eight *Rak'āt*. The first phase is known as *Ṣalātul-Ishrāq* and the second *Ṣalātuḍ-Ḍuḥā*. It has also been named *Ṣalātul-Awwabīn*.

In some Traditions, however, the six *Rak'āt* Prayer offered in between *Maghrib* and *'Ishā'* Prayers is called *Ṣalātul-Awwabīn*.

FUNERAL PRAYER

When it seems that someone is approaching his time of death, the recitation of *Sūrah Yā Sīn* (Ch. 36 of the Holy Quran) is recommended. The reason for this choice is that the topics dealt with in this *Sūrah* are of a nature which alleviate the suffering of the person concerned and give him a kind of spiritual comfort. One should also recite, in low but audible tone, the *Takbīr*, and *Kalimah Shahādah* near the person concerned. Once the person dies, all those who are present and all who come to know of the death later, should recite:

إِنَّا لِلّٰهِ وَإِنَّآ إِلَيْهِ رَاجِعُوْنَ

Transliteration:

Innā lillāhi wa innā ilaihi rāji'ūn.

Translation:

Indeed we are for Allah and it is to Him that we return.

The eyes of the deceased should be closed by hand and a cloth band should be used round his chin and head so that his mouth is closed. Instead of bewailing, one should remain calm and patient and attend to the funeral and burial arrangements.

The body should be bathed in the following manner:

Fresh or lukewarm water should be used to wash the body three times. The practise of the Holy Prophet[sa] was to put some leaves of a *Berī* tree in the water for washing the dead body. First of all, those limbs, which are washed during normal *Wuḍū'* (Ablutions) should be washed though it is not required to pour water in the mouth or nostrils to clean them or to wash the feet. Next the body should be washed, first the right side and then the left. Private parts of the body should remain covered by a cloth. Men alone can bathe male persons and women alone can bathe female persons. The body should then be wrapped in a shroud, which normally is made of an inexpensive white cloth.

The shroud for men consists of three pieces of cloth; a top sheet to cover the top part of the body, a bottom sheet to cover the lower part and a large sheet to cover the whole body from head to feet.

For a female, however, two additional pieces of cloth are used, one for her chest and the other for her head. Islam instructs that one should arrange the burial with utmost simplicity.

A martyr does not need either bathing or the shroud to wrap his body. He should be buried in the clothes he was wearing at the time of death.

After bathing and wrapping the body in a shroud, the body should be carried on shoulders to the place where the Funeral Prayer is to be performed. The Funeral Prayer is held in the open or in a place built for that purpose called *Janāzah Gāh*. Those present for the funeral service should arrange themselves in rows behind the *Imām*. The number of rows should be odd. The *Imām* should occupy a position ahead of the first row and in the middle, with the body of the deceased resting in front of him. The position of the dead body should be such that the right side of the body should be towards the *Ka'bah*.

The *Imām* commences the Prayer by saying *Allāhu Akbar*, i.e. Allah is the Greatest, loudly. The followers say the same in a low tone. The *Imām* then recites *Thanā'* and *Sūrah Al-Fātiḥah* silently. He then says *Allāhu Akbar* without raising his hand. The followers say *Allāhu Akbar* too, but in a low tone.

Then, the whole congregation recites *Durūd* silently. After that the *Imām* says *Allāhu Akbar* for the third time audibly and the particular prayers for the deceased as given below, are recited. The *Imām* then says *Allāhu Akbar* for the fourth time and, turning his face towards the right says *Assalāmu 'Alaikum wa Raḥmatullāh*, and turning his face towards the left repeats the same to mark the end of the Prayer.

The followers, too, say *Assalāmu 'Alaikum wa Raḥmatullāh*, in a low tone and also turn their faces to the right and left.

There is no *Rukū'* or Prostration in the Funeral Prayer. Funeral Prayer in absentia can also be offered for a deceased person, specially for prominent people or in a case when few Muslims have offered the original Funeral Prayer. To offer a Funeral Prayer for a Muslim is obligatory for the body of all Muslims. It is called *Farḍ-i-Kifāyah*. Thus if only a few people offer the Funeral Prayer they are deemed to have done it on behalf of all Muslims. The rest of the Muslim Community is therefore absolved from the obligation of performing the Funeral Prayer.

If the deceased is an adult, male or female, the following Prayer is recited:

اَللّٰهُمَّ اغْفِرْ لِحَيِّنَا وَ مَيِّتِنَا وَ شَاهِدِنَا وَ غَآئِبِنَا وَ صَغِيْرِنَا وَ
كَبِيْرِنَا وَ ذَكَرِنَا وَ اُنْثَانَا۔ اَللّٰهُمَّ مَنْ اَحْيَيْتَهٗ مِنَّا فَاَحْيِهٖ عَلَى
الْاِسْلَامِ وَ مَنْ تَوَفَّيْتَهٗ مِنَّا فَتَوَفَّهٗ عَلَى الْاِيْمَانِ۔ اَللّٰهُمَّ لَا

تَحْرِمْنَا اَجْرَہٗ وَلَا تَفْتِنَّا بَعْدَہٗ

Transliteration:

Allāhumaghfir liḥayyinā wa mayyitinā wa shāhidinā wa ghā'ibinā wa ṣaghīrinā wa kabīrinā, wa Dhakarinā wa unthānā. Allāhumma man aḥyaitahū minnā fa'aḥyihī 'alal-Islām, wa man tawaffaitahū minnā fatawaffahū 'alal-Īmān. Allāhumma lā taḥrimnā ajrahū walā taftinnā ba'dah.

Translation:

O Allah, forgive our living ones and our deceased ones and those of us who are present and those who are absent, and our young ones and our old ones and our males and our females. O Allah, those of us whom Thou grantest life, keep them firm on Islam, and those of us whom Thou causest to die, cause them to die in the faith. Deprive us not, O Allah, of the benefits relating to the deceased and subject us not to trial after him. *(Ibn-e-Mājah Kitābul-Janā'iz, Bābud-Du'ā' fiṣ-Ṣalāti 'alal janāzah, page 107).*

PRAYER FOR A DECEASED MALE CHILD

اَللّٰھُمَّ اجْعَلْہُ لَنَا سَلَفًا وَّفُرُطًا وَّ اجْعَلْہُ لَنَآ اَجْرًا وَّ ذُخْرًا وَّ

اجْعَلْہُ لَنَا شَافِعًا وَّ مُشَفَّعًا

Transliteration:

Allāhummaj'alhu lanā salafan wa furuṭan, waj'alhu lanā ajran wa dhukhran, waj'alhu lanā shāfi'an wa mushaffa'a.

Translation:

O Allah make him our forerunner, and make him, for us, a reward and a treasure, and make him for us a pleader and accept his pleading.

PRAYER FOR A DECEASED FEMALE CHILD

اَللّٰهُمَّ اجْعَلْهَا لَنَا سَلَفًا وَّفُرُطًا، وَذُخْرًا وَّاَجْرًا وَّشَافِعَةً وَّ

مُشَفَّعَةً

Transliteration:

Allāhumaj'alhā lanā salafan wa furuṭan wa dhukhran wa ajran wa shāfi'atan wa mushaffa'ah.

Translation:

O Allah make her our forerunner, and make her, for us, a reward and a treasure, and make her for us a pleader and accept her pleading.

After the Funeral Prayer, the body should be taken to the cemetery for burial without any delay. The coffin should be carried on shoulders and all those who accompany the coffin should take turns in shouldering the coffin. If the body is to be carried to a considerable distance for burial, a vehicle may be used. Those who follow the funeral procession should continue the remembrance of God as well as pray for the forgiveness of the deceased in a low tone.

The grave may be prepared either as a dug up area which contains a further niche (*laḥd*) inside for the body to rest on or it may be just a dug up area. However, it is essential for the grave to be wide and spacious. In extreme cases more than one body can be buried in one grave. If the burial at a particular location is meant to be temporary, or if the burial ground is likely to be affected by flood waters, then it is permissible to use an iron or wooden box for the corpse so as to protect the body from decaying too early.

The body must be lowered into the grave with care and caution.

The following should be recited when the body is being lowerd into the grave:

بِسْمِ اللّٰهِ وَ بِاللّٰهِ عَلٰى مِلَّةِ رَسُوْلِ اللّٰهِ صَلَّى اللّٰهُ عَلَيْهِ وَسَلَّمَ

Transtiteration:

Bismillāhi wa billāhi 'alā millati Rasūlillāhi ṣallallāhu 'alaihi wasallam.

Translation:

In the name of Allah and with his blessings, upon the path set by the conduct of the Messenger of Allah, peace be upon him.

As the body is placed in the grave, the sheet wrap should be loosened a bit at the opening and the face tilted a little towards the *Qiblah*. Some bricks or stone slabs should be used to cover the niche (*laḥd*) and then sand or loose earth should be heaped. The following should be recited on this occasion:

مِنْهَا خَلَقْنٰكُمْ وَ فِيْهَا نُعِيْدُكُمْ وَ مِنْهَا نُخْرِجُكُمْ تَارَةً اُخْرٰى۔

Transliteration:

Minhā khalaqnākum wa fīhā nu'īdukum wa minhā nukhrijukum tāratan ukhrā.

Translation:

We have created you out of this (dust) and we shall return you to it and it is out of the same that we shall revive you in the end.

It is in keeping with the practice of the Holy Prophet[sa] to make the heap of the grave somewhat raised from the ground, i.e. a slight hump-like form.

When the burial ceremony is complete, a brief silent congregational Prayer with raised hands should be made for the forgiveness of the deceased. Then the mourners should leave the cemetery reciting the following:

اَلسَّلَامُ عَلَيْكُمْ وَاِنَّا اِنْ شَاءَ اللّٰهُ بِكُمْ لَلَاحِقُوْنَ۔

Transliteration:

Assalāmu 'alaikum wa innā inshā'allāhu bikum la-lāḥiqūn.

Translation:

Peace be upon you and God willing we are certainly bound to join you.

Condolences must be offered to those related to the deceased.

It is commendable for the near and dear ones, or neighbours, to provide meals to the bereaved family for one time at least.

One must not give in to any superstitions. The condolences and conditions of bereavement should be maintained for three days. After that life should come back to normal. However, the period of bereavement as applicable to the widow of the deceased is four months and ten days. According to the Holy Quran, this is a period to stabilise her mentally and emotionally as women are under a great stress, more so than men in this situation, and they need protection from those who sometimes exploit their helplessness by sympathising at the time when such women are more vulnerable. During this period, a widow should not leave her house except for unavoidable needs. In case the woman is the only earning hand in the family and she has to keep up her job obligations, then she is allowed to go out for the purpose of performing her essential professional responsibilities, without socialising herself.

She may further abstain from wearing make-up, dressing up festively, using perfume or taking part in festive ceremonies. This period should be spent by her in the remembrance of Allah and with patience and gratitude to her Creator.

Glossary of Terms

Adhān: The Islamic call to Prayer.

'Aṣr: The 3rd of the five daily Prayer services, offered any time between the time when the sun starts declining and sunset.

Ta'awwudh: Set words for seeking the protection of God against Satan, recited at the beginning of Prayer.

Tashahhud: A set prayer recited silently at the beginning of the *Qa'dah*, or second Sitting position, in Prayer.

Du'ā'i Qunūt: Arabic name of the special prayer recited in the last *Rak'at* of *Vitr* Prayer.

Durūd: Invocation of blessings upon the Holy Prophet of Islam, Muhammad[sa].

'Īdul-Aḍḥā: The Islamic festival commemorating the obedience to God of Prophet Ibrāhīm[as], (or Abraham), and his son Prophet Ishmael[as].

'Īdul-Fiṭr: The Islamic festival concluding the fasting of the month of Ramadan.

Fajr: The 1st of the five daily Prayer services, offered any time during the period starting from dawn and ending a few minutes before sunrise.

Farā'iḍ: Plural form of *Farḍ*.

Farḍ (plural ***Farā'iḍ***): Compulsory or obligatory, used when describing categories of Prayers or constituent parts of Prayer.

***Farḍ-i-Kifāyah*:** Obligatory duty binding on all Muslims, but which is deemed to have been discharged (by all of them), when a body from among them perform it; e.g. the funeral Prayer of a Muslim.

***Fiṭrānah*:** Money contributed by Muslims before the *'Īdul-Fiṭr* Prayer service and spent on the needy so that they may also join in festivities.

***Ḥajj*:** Pilgrimage to the *Ka'bah* in Makkah, Arabia; also known as the fifth pillar of Islam.

Imām: The person who leads a congregational Prayer service.

***Iqāmah*:** A shortened verse of the *Adhān*, which is recited loudly to indicate that a congregational Prayer is about to start. See also *Takbīr*.

***'Ishā'*:** The 5th and last of the five daily Prayer services, offered any time between nightfall and midnight, or before going to bed.

***Jilsah*:** The Sitting position which occurs in between two prostrations during Prayer.

***Kalimah*:** The credo of Islam, There is none worthy of worship except Allah; Muhammad is the Messenger of Allah.

Kalimah Shahādah (also called *Kalimah*): The declaration of Islamic faith, i.e. to bear witness that there is none worthy of worship except Allah, He is One, without any associate, and to bear witness that Muhammad is the servant and Messenger of Allah.

***Khusūf*:** Eclipse of the moon, during which a special

Prayer is to be offered.

Kusūf **:** Eclipse of the sun, during which a special prayer is to be offered.

Maghrib**:** The 4th of the five daily Prayer services, which can be offered any time in the period starting from immediately after sunset and ending when there is still some light left on the horizon.

Makrūhāt**:** Acts which are considered undesirable or below the dignity of Prayer.

Mālikīs**:** One of the sects of Islam.

Mu'adhdhin**:** The person who says the *Adhān*, or Call to Prayer.

Mustaḥab: (plural *Mustaḥibbāt*): Preferable or praiseworthy things, when referring to the style or manner of performing Prayer.

Nawāfil**:** Optional or supererogatory as applied to types or categories of Prayer.

Niyyah**:** The Formal intention which one makes in one's mind before starting a Prayer.

Qa'dah**:** Sitting position adopted towards the end of the second *Rak'at* in Prayer.

Qaḍā**:** Offering a missed Prayer.

Qaṣr**:** The act of shortening one's Prayer.

Qaumah**:** The posture of Standing erect after *Rukū'*.

Qiyām**:** The standing position in Prayer.

Rak'at**:** One complete unit within Prayer, consisting of a number of different postures of the body with corresponding prescribed prayers, words of glorification and of praise of God.

***Rak'āt*:** Plural form of *Rak'at.*

***Rukū'*:** The Bowing down position in Prayer.

***Sajdah*:** (*Sujūd*) The position of Prostration in prayer.

***Ṣalātul-Jumu'ah*:** The Friday prayer service.

***Ṣalāt*:** Prayer in the prescribed form; also known as the second pillar of Islam.

***Ṣalātul-Ḥājjāt*:** Prayer offered when one is in need or in difficulty *Ṣalātul-Ishrāq*: Optional Prayer offered in two phases in the forenoon.

Ṣalātuḍ-Ḍuḥā: The second phase of *Ṣalātul-Ishrāq*.

***Ṣaum*:** Fasting in the month of *Ramadan*; also known as the fourth pillar of Islam.

***Shias*:** One of the sects of Islam.

***Sujūd*: (*Sajdah*):** The posture of Prostration in Prayer.

***Sujūdus-Sahv*:** Prostrations of condonement performed when a mistake has been committed during Prayer and which may affect its validity.

***Sunan*:** Plural form of *Sunnat.*

***Sunnah* or *Sunnat*:** One of the types or categories of Prayer; less compulsory than a *Farḍ* (obligatory) Prayer, but more so than a *Nawāfil* (voluntary) one.

***Sunnis*:** One of the sects of Islam.

***Sūrah*:** Arabic word for 'chapter', and used for designating the chapters of the Holy Quran.

***Sutra*:** An object which a worshipper places before him to mark the physical boundary of his Prayer.

***Tahajjud*:** Optional Prayer of great merit offered in the latter part of the night.

***Taḥmī'*:** The prescribed words recited by the congregation in response to the *Tasmī'* of the *Imām*; also, words of praise and remembrance of God.

***Takbīr*:** A set formula, recited loudly in order to indicate that a congregational Prayer is about to start.

***Takbīr-i-Taḥrīmah*:** The Arabic expression *Allāhu Akbar* (God is the Greatest), proclaimed loudly by the *Imām* while he raises his two hands to his earlobes at the very beginning of a congregational Prayer service.

***Tarāvīḥ*:** Special Prayer offered after *'Ishā'* Prayer during the month of Ramadan.

www.ingramcontent.com/pod-product-compliance
Lightning Source LLC
Chambersburg PA
CBHW071522080526
44588CB00011B/1526
* 9 7 8 1 8 4 8 8 0 8 5 6 0 *